KITS
FOR
KIDS

Nancy Towner Butterworth
Laura Peabody Broad
Illustrations by Penny Carter

KITS FOR KIDS

Projects to do, gifts to give, experiences to share with children age 3 and up

ST. MARTIN'S PRESS • New York

Also by the authors:
The Playgroup Handbook

Copyright © 1980 by Nancy Towner Butterworth and Laura Peabody Broad
Illustrations copyright © 1980 by Penny Carter
ST. MARTIN'S PRESS
175 Fifth Avenue
New York, N.Y. 10010

Manufactured in the United States of America

Library of Congress Cataloging in Publication Data

Butterworth, Nancy Towner.
  Kits for kids.

  SUMMARY: Suggests craft projects for a variety
of occasions.
  1.   Handicraft.   [1.   Handicraft]   I.   Broad,
Laura Peabody, joint author.   II.   Title.
TT157.B84   745.5   80–14545
ISBN 0–312–45701–4
ISBN 0–312–45702–2 (pbk.)

Dedication

To good times shared with our own children,
Neil, Craig,
Kenneth, Laurie, and Douglas,
and to
Julie Andrews
whose love for life has left
us gifts to remember

Laurie

Craig

Doug

Ken

neil

Acknowledgments

We are grateful to many friends, parents and teachers who have worked with children of all ages and have shared their experiences with us.

We thank the members of the AAUW Parenting Group of Western Springs who will recognize some of their "Brainstorming" ideas on these pages. We also thank La Grange PACES and other child care groups which have also lent some of their thoughts.

Much helpful professional advice has been offered by elementary teachers, nursery school directors and day care providers through Teachers Room store located in Needham, Massachusetts.

We also thank our editor, Barbara Anderson, who has given us her critical eye, some good activity ideas and her patient guidance.

Contents

Introduction

Part I.   New Ways to Plan, Present, and Use Activities   1

     Chapter 1. Creating Activities   3
        The Simplest Way to Plan Activities   4
        Creating Activities from Subjects   4
        Creating Activities from Materials   5
            Groupings of Materials • Single Items • Bits
            and Scraps • Materials Free and Bought •
            Store Bought Articles and Surprise Kits •
            Materials on Loan • Starter and Add-to Sets
        Tailoring Activities to Children's Needs   9

     Chapter 2. Presenting Activities in New Ways   11
        Inexpensive Ideas for Packaging   12
        When You Do Not Want to Wrap   13
        Ideas for Making and Using Directions for Activities   13

     Chapter 3. Ways to Use Activity Kits   15
        Who Can Use Activity Kits and When   15
            Parents • Sitters • Grandparents • Friends •
            Group Leaders • Teachers • Children
        Sharing Gifts and Experiences   20
        The Child Alone   21

Part II. Kits to use at Home   23

        Chapter 4. Using Kits at Home   25
             Quick Kits   27
             Activity Kits   31

Part III. Kits to Use in a Group   55

        Chapter 5. Using Kits in a Group   57
             Quick Kits   60
             Activity Kits   66

Part IV. Kits for Special Occasions   91

        Chapter 6. Using Kits for Special Occasions   93
             Quick Kits   96
             Activity Kits   102

Part V. Kits for Confined Situations   127

        Chapter 7. Using Kits for Confined Situations   129
             Quick Kits   132
             Activity Kits   137

Part VI. Kits for Going Places   161

        Chapter 8. Using Kits for Going Places   163
             Quick Kits   167
             Activity Kits   172

Appendix I.   Activities by Type   195
Appendix II.   Activities by Skill   202
Appendix III. Activities Especially Suitable for Use by Parents, Grandparents, Older Siblings and Sitters, Preschoolers, Teachers, Small Organized Groups, and Day Care Centers   205

Table of Contents

At-Home Quick Kits

Arts and Crafts Kits

  Linoleum Block Prints   27

  Vegetable Sculptures   28

Dramatic Play Kits

  Pup Tent   28

Game Kits

  Squeeze-Bottle Squirt Play   29

  Tin Can Golf   29

Science Kits

  Bathtub Scientist   30

  Invisible Ink   30

  Weather Bureau   30

Miscellaneous Kits

  Nothing-to-Do Jar   29

At-Home Activity Kits

Arts and Crafts Kits

  Kitchen-Made Sand Art   51

  Magnet Art   32

  Pom-Pom Making   33

  Thumb-and-Fingerprint Doodles   35

Cooking Kits

  Easy Pizza Making   38

  M and M Party Cookies   37

  Root Beer Making   40

Dramatic Play Kits

  Army-Navy Camp-out Pretend   45

  Do-Your-Thing   41

Game Kits

  Masking Tape Floor Games   48

  Bag-of-Labels Make-a-Game   50

Science Kits

  Heavy Things Sink   31

  Take Apart   53

Woodworking Kits

  Carpenter's Tool Kit   43

  Make a Table   46

Quick Kits for Groups

Arts and Crafts Kits

  Instant Wall Hanging   65

  Tissue Paper Stained Glass   61

Cooking Kits

  Instant S'mores   60

Dramatic Play Kits

  Actress Pretend   62

Game Kits

  Ring-the-Bell Game   60

Science Kits

  Bird Nest Building Bag   63

  Pond Adventure   63

  Mystery Smelling Jars   64

  Weigh Things   64

Woodworking Kits

  Mini Carpenter Kit   65

  Scene Building Blocks   60

  Whittling Fuzz Sticks   62

Activity Kits for Groups

Arts and Crafts Kits

Fingerpaint Fun 66
Quilt-Making Iron-On Crayon 72

Cooking Kits

Best Ever Cocoa Making 67
Metric Snack 80

Dramatic Play Kits

Big-Mouth Disguise 70

Game Kits

Follow the Footsteps 76
Olympic Games 90
Tape Resist Game Board 88

Music Kits

Rhythm Art 78
Strumming 79

Science Kits

Mystery Feely Box 75
Narcissus Planting 69
Pringle's Bug Catcher 82

Storytelling Kits

Clothesline Story and Display 84

Woodworking Kits

Log Bird Feeder 86
Napkin Holder 87

Quick Kits for Special Occasions

Arts and Crafts Kits

Bag of Clay 96
May Day Pin Basket 97
School Photo Bookmark 101
Wooden Spoon Boutique Gift 96

Cooking Kits

Ice-Cream-Cone Clowns 98
Speedy Birthday Cake 100

Dramatic Play Kits

Mystery Purse 101

Game Kits

Heidi's Paper Bag Piñata 98
Party Favor Bag 99

Science Kits

Flame Color Mix 99
Violet-by-Mail Surprise 100

Miscellaneous Kits

Jelly Bean Taste Test 97

Activity Kits for Special Occasions

Arts and Crafts Kits

Activity or Recipe Box 102
Collage Memories 103
Family Bouquet 110
Make Your Own Cards 112
Personalized Pencil Case or Book Bag 105

Cooking Kits

Candy House 106
Cookie Cutter Knox Blox 109
Spook Salad-Making 104

Dramatic Play Kits

Clown 114
Robot Costume 116

Game Kits

Floor Pool Game 118

Party Kits

Fireside 119
Party Game 120

Service Kits

Lighten-Your-Load Help 122

Woodworking Kits

Stompers 'n' Stilts 123

Quick Kits for Confined Situations

Arts and Crafts Kits

Crayon Rubbings	135
Playdough Marble Roll Game	132
Patchwork Scribbles	134

Game Kits

Color Play	133
Map Fun	132
Spotlight Game	136

Science Kits

Light-Up Electric Fun	133
Magnifying Magic	134

Storytelling Kits

Recording	136
Photo Album	132
Squiggle Story Notebook	136

Woodworking Kits

Work-and-Play Project Board	135

Activity Kits for Confined Situations

Arts and Crafts Kits

Cloth Flowers	138
Miniature Scene	140
Plant a Desert	142
Sewing Card	144
Sparkling Window Shade Pulls	146

Cooking Kits

Paintbrush Cookies	148

Dramatic Play Kits

Paper Doll Set Design	147

Game or *Music Kits*

Guess the Sounds and Tunes	137

Science Kits

Bird Watching	149
Flashlight Planetarium	151
Shell Identification	153

Storytelling Kits

Felt-Board Tepee	156
Newspaper Boat Folding	158

Woodworking Kits

Hang-Your-Jewels Holder	152
Wood Pieces	154

Quick Kits for Going Places
Arts and Crafts Kits
  Rub-On Fantasy   167
  Stencil Art   167
Cooking Kits
  String a Snack   170
Dramatic Play Kits
  Microphone Play   168
  Pretend Binoculars   171
Game Kits
  Black and Red Cards   168
  Dice Decide   168
  Jump Rope and Jingle Book   169
  Preschooler's Purse   170
  Unlock!   171
Storytelling Kits
  Book Countdown   169
  Listen!   169

Activity Kits for Going Places
Arts and Crafts Kits
  Autograph Clipboard   173
  Berry-Picking Basket   174
  Cross-Stitch on Gingham   177
  Mini Sewing Kit   180
Cooking Kits
  Grandma Stoklosa's Cookie Mix   176
Game Kits
  Battleship Game   182
  Clipboard Pencil and Paper Games   191
Science Kits
  Color Tester   172
Travel Entertainment Kits
  Collection Starter   185
  Explore Grab Bag   186
  Going-Places Surprise   188
Miscellaneous Kits
  Mini Emergency Kit   184
  New Neighbor Get-Acquainted Kit   179

*An asterisk next to an item listed in a kit's "materials" section indicates that the item is common to most homes and need not be included in the kit package.

Introduction

K *its for Kids* is a new kind of activity book. It is an idea book that can be used as a handy reference by *everyone* in the family and anyone who lives or works with children. It is primarily concerned with new ways to plan and present activities and new ways to use them. It shows how to put materials together so they inspire children to try new things. It also shows how to make creative learning experiences a part of routine living so that the demands of many different kinds of situations can be met.

If you are a parent, group leader, or teacher, chances are you're continually looking for original projects to use with the children around you. This book suggests creative ways to combine various materials to invent new activities. Just as a toy manufacturer assembles a selection of items to make a science kit, magic kit, or handicraft kit, you can put together a grouping of different objects to produce an imaginative homemade "kit," designed to meet the needs of a particular child or group of children. Such original sets can be devised to lead to a wide range of experiments, creative learning experiences,

and the development of new skills. Hints are given here on how to brainstorm for original activity ideas and how to combine a wide range of materials for making unique projects.

If you have children or work with children, you are probably acutely aware that the way an activity is presented can make all the difference in whether a child wants to try it. In this book you'll find inventive ways to present new things to do. One approach is to take a cue from successful toy makers who, by clever packaging, turn straightforward projects into I-can't-wait-to-do-it surprises. Original packages and wrappings can be fun to create and can help generate enthusiasm for testing new skills and creative work. Within these pages are a variety of suggestions for the novel presentation of activities.

Using activities effectively is another challenge. A project need not be something to do when there is nothing else to do. Different day-to-day situations lend themselves to different kinds of activities. Children's creative learning projects can become a part of the fabric of daily living.

Children of various ages play together.

People of all generations interact. Parents, teachers, and other adults plan for special circumstances. During times of illness a child's attention must be diverted or when a sitter comes the child needs to be made to feel at ease. The list of times when an appropriate project can be slipped in to fill a need of the moment is virtually endless. This book is full of tips for fitting the activity to the situation.

A major portion of *Kits for Kids* puts lots of easy-to-use activities at your fingertips. These activities are divided according to different day-to-day situations for use At Home, In a Group, On Special Occasions, In Confined Situations, and Going Places. Some are familiar ideas that should be a part of any "how to" activity library. Many are new ideas combined with elements of the old and familiar, so there is plenty of room for experimenting and creating on the part of the doer.

There is an assortment of activities that are quick to do and require only a handful of materials which can be easily popped into a paper bag and given as an impromptu surprise. We call these "Quick Kits." In addition, there is a large collection of more involved activities that have universal appeal.

A wide variety of subject areas is represented, from crafts, cooking, and science, to woodworking, music, and dramatic play. Each activity indicates the ages for appropriate use and the skills that it develops and reinforces. Each activity points out the kinds of times when the project might fill a particular need, like the moment when a snappy game is required for diversion in the dentist's waiting room or when a unique gift is needed to welcome a new neighbor.

Each activity provides a complete list of materials and clear directions written in words to be understood by elementary school children. Appealing ideas for creating packaging and presenting directions have been included for use when the set of project materials is going to be given as a gift.

Both Nancy Butterworth and Laura Broad hold master's degrees in education and are experienced elementary school teachers. They are the co-authors of *Playgroup Handbook,* a book of activities for preschoolers. President of the local Board of Education, Nancy Butterworth has been involved in the organization and running of nursery schools. Laura Broad has done a television mini-series on projects for children and managed a home day care program. Both have conducted workshops on working with children for an assortment of parenting groups and other organizations. While this experience has provided a solid background for putting together a book such as this, the authors' most important qualification is that they are both mothers sharing learning experiences with their own children, who range in age from seven to fourteen.

The material in this book comes largely from the authors' own experience with children. The activities have in large part been done with children or groups of children with whom they have worked. They have supplemented their ideas with those of other mothers and teachers and have referred to activity books to strengthen specific areas.

NEW WAYS TO PLAN, PRESENT, AND USE ACTIVITIES

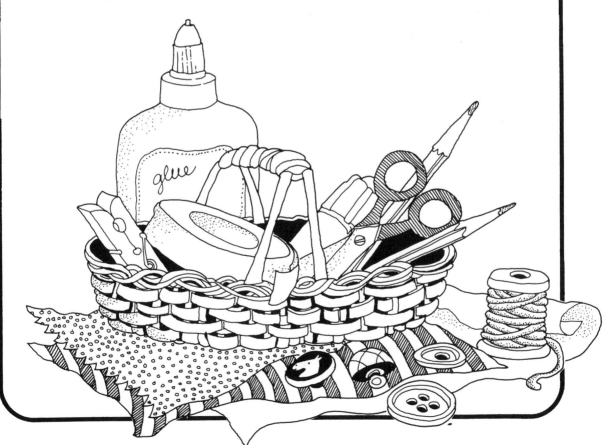

Chapter 1

Creating Activities

There are many times when the parent, teacher, or group leader needs to have an activity or gift handy—to fill an unexpected free moment, to celebrate a special occasion, or to suit a given situation. There are also blocks of time when it is important to have some worthwhile activities planned for children. It makes sense for you to set materials aside for special projects and to have a few ideas for spur of the moment fun tucked up your sleeve.

A few creative surprises on the shelf can be a godsend to the parent whose time is at a premium or to the teacher who needs novel ways to challenge her class and new spare-time activities for the fast workers in her group. Original ideas are always welcome to group leaders seeking fresh ways to inspire enthusiastic learning and play.

You can create projects to add variety to children's play. Through home-assembled sets of materials children can become familiar with untried sources of entertainment and learning such as the kitchen, workshop, or sewing corner. They are no longer confined to the toy box and TV set. Being involved with such projects can push a child's imagination in fresh creative directions. For example, inventing a new game or making a discovery about animal life near his own doorstep can give a child a real feeling of achievement and a sense of having contributed to his own fun.

There are many different ways to put together activity ideas. Numerous combinations of themes and materials can be shaped to meet the special needs of an individual child or a specific situation. The pages ahead will suggest some of the possibilities.

The Simplest Way to Plan Activities

The simplest way for you to create an activity is to draw from the specific ideas in this book. The Quick Kits listed in each section of Part II involve few supplies and a minimum of explanation. You can just toss the materials into a bag and give them to a child with verbal or written directions. Try some of these for your first homemade project experiences—then try some of the slightly more involved activities that follow. With the longer projects use materials listed as your "shopping list." Collect the supplies that you already have at home and then complete the list on your next trip to the store.

Other sources of inspiration for simple project kits are hobby shops, toy stores, and gift catalogs. Look at ready-made kits while you are shopping, or browse through a catalog or two. You will see lots of simple, boxed activities such as basic craft kits or uncomplicated games. Many are easy to duplicate. You can look at the contents, make "shopping lists" from them, then put together your own.

Even seemingly complex toys or games can often be copied. A close look may reveal a straightforward game souped up with plastic, flashing lights, and a big price tag! The game Battleship is a case in point. It is available in an expensive, elaborate set using pegs for bombarding opponent's ships. It is also available at lower cost in preprinted pages with directions. For still less money and with the same amount of fun you can produce the game with a pad of graph paper and a pencil (see *Battleship*, p. 182).

Creating Activities from Subjects

Your own imagination can lead you to a variety of activity ideas. You might begin with a subject as the basis for a brainstorm. Cooking, magic, music, or sewing are just a few of the areas that might have special appeal for you or the children for whom you are planning.

For cooking, you might decide on a basket containing the ingredients and recipe for a kitchen experiment such as *Root Beer Making Kit* (p. 40); for magic, how about a deck of cards (not necessarily brand new) with directions for a magic card trick or two? For a musical experience you might bring together two or more elements such as a record, a homemade instrument (or materials to make one), and a costume from cast-off clothing to inspire a dance performance or dramatic play. A simple sewing kit might be a coffee tin into which you have tucked yarn, needle, and fabric for experimenting with basic stitches. The possibilities are endless.

When you have a subject in mind, but your own inventiveness needs a boost, flip to Appendix I for a handy listing by type of activities listed in this book.

Creating Activities from Materials

Groupings of Materials. A set of materials can often become the inspiration for creative ideas. Children learn through exposure to a diversity of substances and objects, and they will enjoy experimenting with all sorts of materials ranging from the usual paint and crayons to objects gathered from nature. You can combine simple art supplies like pad, crayons, and stencil in a gift to inspire creativity. These selections might give rise to early spelling attempts or experiments in design. A set including dried weeds, sand, and a few shells could prompt other kinds of imaginative adventures, such as the making of a centerpiece to adorn the kitchen table or miniature sandbox shell play.

An engaging game for adults and children alike is to think of two or three common objects and dream up as many ideas for using them as the mind can imagine! An enthusiastic parenting group tested their imaginations this way by conjuring up new creative play ideas for their children. With a selection of pennies, glue, and boxes they devised penny toss games, a bank made from a box decorated with glued-on pennies, a pretend-story about a "good penny" and a "bad penny," an experiment with sound that involved dropping pennies into a box from different heights—and more. The possibilities suggested by those few common items seemed virtually limitless.

Another set of items for the group's consideration was straws, ping pong balls, and markers. These brought forth such ideas as a game in which two children blow through straws to pass the ping pong ball back and forth, a science demonstration of a miniature version of wind, and an exercise in art and dramatic play with faces drawn on ping pong ball characters!

Try this game yourself. Bring together a few mundane objects and come up with ideas of your own for using them. Share your ideas with the children; then let them glide off into their own flights of creative fancy to find more ways for using the articles.

Here is a sample brainstorming list from which to choose your two or three objects. Pop a few of them in a paper sack, tie with a bow, and you have a creative gift —a Quick Kit:

Brainstorm List			
sand	old snapshots	pennies	rubber bands
dried weeds	markers	ping pong ball	glue
masking tape	gift-wrapping tubes	string	shells
box	clay	buttons	
straws	scissors	cardboard or paper scraps	

You can bring together larger items to invent creative play and learning just as successfully and in combinations that you won't find at the local toy store. Join a speciality item with a book to initiate dramatic play along with a whole range of other experiences. For example, a top hat and a book of magic given together can turn the recipient into a performer in costume with magic tricks at hand to try. Perhaps the young magician will share his new-found talents by entertaining at his sister's birthday party!

The *Do-Your-Thing Kit* (p. 41) gives several examples of ways to bring together costumes, (and) books, or other materials in a terrific learning and gift idea that certainly beats last minute buying of a stereotyped toy! You will enjoy experimenting with your own combinations for custom-made project kits, too.

Single Item. Sometimes a single material can inspire a whole toy box of pleasures. A good example is a plain roll of masking tape. Using a formica counter top for a surface, a very young child might find himself engaged in laying out a network of tape roads for his tiny cars, or marking off squares for a game of tic tac toe. He might use these and other inventions for play on the back floor of the station wagon or on an old game board. Older children could use the tape for more complicated games such as hopscotch or hockey (p. 48) with boundaries taped to the carpeted floor. They might fashion designs or letters by sticking tape on diverse surfaces.

This one versatile item entertains all ages and is equally appealing when used by a child alone or in a group. It is adaptable to a variety of situations from a day of sickness to party entertainment and even fills the bill when a child becomes impatient waiting for a friend to arrive to play. Give this or another single item with a lead-off suggestion or two. One simple material can be the source of hours of play.

Here are a few of the single items that can prompt many possibilities for improvisation: a paper punch; a piece of clay; straws to glue together, blow through, or drink with; or beans from the kitchen shelf for counting games, rhythm instruments, drop art, mosaics, bean bags. Try making a brainstorming list to come up with new ideas for what to do with single items just as you did with the sets of common objects.

While something you have around the house may be the source of creative play, perhaps an item somewhere else will catch your eye and trigger a fresh idea. For example, you might spot some of those funny jiggly eyes in the hobby shop. Pop these in a box labeled "Creature Kit," toss in glue, scissors, fabric and paper scraps, cotton balls, or whatever and you have a great surprise kit offering endless possibilities for creature making.

Wherever you are—at a garage sale, on the beach, in a flea market, or on a mountain path—something is near you that can trigger creative thinking and doing. Keep your imagination alive and open to all the possibilities.

Bits and Scraps. It is evident that many of the supplies for activities are simply articles you have readily available. Often the materials can be discarded scraps and bits ripe for recycling. Rebottling leftover paints from the workbench may be just what is required to round out a building kit. Using scraps from the sewing box may make a handiwork kit a real bargain.

A cast-off sock, buttons, fabric pieces, needle, and thread arranged in a box marked "Puppet-Making Project" make a great rainy-day surprise. It is a good way to divert attention from the TV set and not spend a penny.

If you will take just ten minutes longer when you are winding up a project of your own, the results can be the making of a gift kit ready to package and personalize for giving. While those pinking shears are still out, why not cut fabric and paper squares for doll-size quilt making (p. 72)? When you are in the middle of a wood project, why not cut some wood scraps to size for the makings of several simple boats?

Materials Free and Bought. You can easily combine a purchased item with home discards to make a toy with potential for more creative play. A fad item might catch your eye in a store—perhaps a super hero doll—and you know it would capture the fancy of a child, too. Purchase it, add a few simple materials, for example masking tape and a few boxes, and you will have inexpensively added a new dimension to the toy.

A child may turn a shoe box into Superman's telephone-booth dressing room, or he might tape several boxes together to simulate skyscrapers in the "Great Metropolis." You could have bought a super hero kit with a ready-made building, but at a high price, and you would have a toy lacking the creative flexibility that the unmarked boxes and tape provide.

Turn to the *Miniature Scene Kit* (p. 140) for a working example of how a useless but appealing object, a miniature animal, becomes the reason for arts and crafts fun.

Brand new things come together with on-hand materials to make happy, creative combinations. Tune in to ways to expand the use of old and new toys with the addition of free, readily available materials.

Store-Bought Articles and Surprise Kits. Some kits that you assemble will be comprised entirely of store-bought articles. They might be a combination of items, such as popsicle sticks or coffee stirrers, new glue, and a brush for miniature house making, or beads and pipe cleaners for making *Sparkling Window Shade Pulls* (p. 146).

Other times the parts of your set might be a couple of objects that, used together, will hint at certain kinds of play. For instance, the canteen and backpack from the *Army-Navy Camp-out Pretend Kit* (p. 45) might suggest an outdoor sleepover or a picnic.

Coordinating store purchases can be a real shopping spree for your imagination. How about packaging a new flashlight with a poster for a hospital gift? The patient can dream up his own games to play using the two things together or separately. For example, he might use the flashlight to "spotlight" parts of the wall-hung poster picture (p. 136).

A trip to a hardware store might give you a chance to choose elements for a gift to turn a timid three-year-old into a self-assured *Bathtub Scientist* (p. 30), or to purchase a couple of *real* tools for a budding mechanic (p. 43).

Kits made up of an assortment of inexpensive store-bought toys and learning materials are fun to assemble. They can make great Surprise Kits (p. 188). They can provide a number of things to do over a long period of time. A stroll through the dime store and stationer's may produce a potpourri of little items such as pocket games, hole punchers, paper and pad with carbon, and toy cars. All are stocking-stuffer-type items that would be great for whiling away hours in a sick bed or on a long car trip. These cost more money than home-assembled bits and scraps, but you can put together a good variety that gives a lot more play and learning mileage than, say, a big stuffed animal.

If you do assemble a Surprise Kit, aim for a balanced variety of items. Paper work and drawing wear thin after awhile! Miniature toy play could get boring. A good combination for such a surprise kit might include a game for solitary play; a game to play with someone else; a toy for pretending, such as a puppet or doll; and something for paper work, such as stencils or carbon paper. Include, too, a craft item that can be managed in a confined setting, perhaps an activity and materials for doing it chosen from this book.

Surprise Kits can be as simple or elaborate as you wish to make them. Design them to fit your particular needs and budget, and package them cleverly. For the preschooler, using an old purse full of special compartments would be an appealing bag from which to "grab" and a good place to store surprises after opening. A converted closet shoe bag can uniquely organize grab activities for a child confined to bed.

Materials on Loan. Sometimes you want to give a child an experience or gift that requires the use of an overly expensive tool or rarely used piece of equipment. What a pity to let that stand in the way! A simple loan can often solve the problem. Let the selection of objects include the necessary materials plus the loan of or arrangements for the use of that major item.

For example, a tape recorder and tapes on loan (p. 136) will allow free trial of an expensive surprise perfect for entertaining children in confined situations. The loan of a pair of binoculars along with a bird identification book may spark an interest in birdwatching (p. 149) and make it clear whether an investment in binoculars would be worthwhile.

Ten-year-old Laurie was delighted when she found she could afford to share her interest in linoleum block printing with a friend confined for a week with chicken pox. She purchased a new linoleum block and one color ink for under two dollars. Then she wrapped up her own cutting tools and paint roller and marked them "on loan." Her homemade gift kit not only made a practical get well thought, but also, by combining a purchase and a loan, made possible the sharing of a new experience. The loan made that experience possible.

So many times children are eager to try something new. A momentary investment is often made when sustained interest is lacking. Homemade project kits with a loan bonus allow a child to test out his interest before spending large amounts of money.

Starter and Add-to Sets. Starter and Add-to gift kits serve a similiar trial purpose. Children often become fired with enthusiasm for stamp collecting, camping, or any number of other pursuits. The ideal way to meet such inspired interest is with a starter or add-to kit. Such kits may be bought pre-assembled but it is cheaper to put together your own and in doing so you have control over the contents.

A few pennies, a penny display page, and coin identification book may start someone on the road to a life long hobby. One or two pieces of camping equipment may lead to a love of "roughing it," then again, maybe not! The experiment might be fun but brief, and not worth further investments. If the interest lasts, then the signal is "go" and more parts to the starter kit may be added.

Tailoring Activities to Children's Needs

Whatever your plans may be for collecting materials and assembling kits, your prime focus should be the children themselves. Your plans should take into account their ages, skills, interests, and special needs. In creating productive kit experiences you will need to keep in mind that the child should work as independently as possible and be encouraged to contribute his or her own ideas to the process.

Obviously a younger child's skills will not be as highly developed as those of an older child. A four-year-old who still has difficulty with small motor coordination will need to have a tricky step in a project pre-done for him. His ten-year-old sister may enjoy exactly the same activity, but she will be able to do it in its entirety. For example, both children will enjoy *Flashlight Planetarium* (p. 151). For the preschooler you would pre-punch a star formation so that he can have fun flashing the light through the holes. His older sister would be able to refer to a constellation book and punch her own stars. Together they can use their homemade planetariums to help them locate constellations in the night sky.

Children of different ages working together may complement each other by giving help to one another in areas in which they are most proficient. For example an older brother might be persuaded to prepare a *Pringles Bug Catcher Kit* (p. 82) for a younger child's friends or playgroup. The group enjoys the hunting and capturing of a variety of living creatures. The older child expresses interest in the habits of the captured bugs, sharing observations and sparking an interest in the others. The younger children take his lead in observing the creatures. The bossiness that so often appears when older children help younger children can dissipate in the combined enthusiasm over the project at hand.

Even within a given age group children display vast differences in their range of skills. Consider the age, but also consider the abilities of a given child. Some five-year-olds, for example, may be very proficient at cutting. A child at seven, capable in every other way, may have small motor problems that make handling scissors very difficult. If cutting is the problem, whatever the child's age, then adjust accordingly. Adapt a cut-and-paste activity by tucking some precut pieces into the kit and making sure blunt scissors are available.

Children vary in their ability to concentrate. Are you planning a gift kit for someone with a very short attention span? Plan something for him that gives effective results but is satisfyingly quick to do, or give him a project that can be picked up, put down and worked on periodically without much mess. This child will do poorly in a sit-and-wait kind of situation. If you are arranging a project in confined circumstances, try to build some movement into the plan.

Of course, you will be thinking of a child's likes and interests when you organize an activity kit for him. What are his enthusiasms? Maybe he is a real shell freak. Great! A bag of shells you collected is perfect for him, and the addition of a shell identification book will be the touch that really helps him expand his interest. See *Shell Identification* (p. 153).

Confronted with a youngster with a preference for cooking, you might design an activity that stretches this interest into the realm of science by presenting some ideas for testing the senses of taste and smell.

An ill or incapacitated child presents a special challenge. What can you do for the woodworking fan or athletic enthusiast who is frustratingly confined to bed? For the woodworker, it is time to forgo the hammer, but a sack of wood pieces and some glue can put him in the bedroom woodworking business. The bedridden athlete? Hand him a bag with all the ingredients to make scrunched paper balls and number marked boxes for scoring. Line the score boxes at the foot of the bed and the patient can toss the balls. *Voila!* "Bed Basketball!"

Every child is different. His needs and interests are unique. Always keep in mind the needs and likes of the child or children when you are choosing the subjects and materials for the activities.

Chapter 2

Presenting Activities in New Ways

Toymakers know that clever packaging adds eye appeal. A gift in a unique container or disguised in a wrapped box captures immediate interest and inspires a desire to undo the contents and try what is inside. Part of the fun of gift giving is the element of surprise created by clever packaging and wrapping. Dressing up a set of materials with paper and bow can add a sense of importance to an occasion.

There are many times when you will need gifts specially done up for birthdays, holidays, or when a reward is in order. There are also other times when thoughtful recognition is appropriate. Putting together a few carefully selected elements will allow you to plan creative sharing for such times. A box and bow can make an everyday occurrence seem very special indeed. You might indulge in expensive wrappings for calendar holidays but the cost of attractive store-bought gift decorations might diminish your enthusiasm for dressing up packages for the more impromptu gift-giving occasions. It seems simpler just to set out materials ready to use. Why bother to bundle everything together into a package? Is it really necessary to wrap at such times? Of course it isn't, but an appealing pail of objects or items showcased in a box with bow says, "I'm special. Try me!" When you think up activities for children you have become your own toy "manufacturer." With simple packaging you can add to projects the elements of glamour, mystery, and anticipation that so appeal to children. *And* you can save money in the bargain!

By prepackaging a few activity ideas, you'll always have some presents on hand for those frequent birthday parties your child attends. If you are a working mother or single parent, it is a help to have some special projects laid aside to pull out and do or wrap as a gift. Any parent appreciates a solution to the moment when no toy in the drawers seems to satisfy. A ready-packed activity encircled in eye-catching ribbon can turn a restless period into a time of fun and learning.

If you are a group leader or teacher, challenged to motivate your charges, activities presented as "gifts" can encourage fresh enthusiasm in the group. An added twist to the packaging idea might be to wrap the parts of a new activity separately so several members of the group can take part in the unveiling!

Inexpensive Ideas for Packaging

You can turn kit packaging into a game by always being on the lookout for simple and inexpensive materials. Use your own creative imagination along with the fresh ideas contributed by your children. Here are a few ideas to help you along.

The accumulation of items in our own homes provides a storehouse from which to draw. Take a look around. What do you have to use for handy containers? Pull-string bags, lidded boxes, brown grocery bags, and handled shopping bags all pass into your household in the course of a year. All are ready-made for recycling into your own packaging operation. There are also those assorted boxes and tins that can be dressed up with contact paper, fabric scraps, or wallpaper. Paper paint buckets or cheap plastic buckets are great for tossing in the ingredients for a project. Buckets from fast food concessions or ice cream chain stores serve equally well. Transparent shoe boxes make real showcases for gifts.

A garage sale is a great source for inexpensive packaging. Imagine finding a mixing bowl and using it to house the ingredients for a kitchen activity kit, or finding a basket to hold the cookie cutters and ingredients for a cookie-making project. The basket or bowl could be used later for serving the freshly made cookies or other project goodies.

Many items can be recycled and used for wrapping. Newspaper and magazine pages are inexpensive and can attractively personalize packages. Sometimes you can find a page that suits the theme of the gift and gives a clue to the contents. A tempting food ad in bright color becomes a cooking project wrap. The sports page disguises the materials for a game of skill. Maybe you want the contents to remain a complete mystery and so you select newspaper or magazine pages appropriate to the age, interest, or hobbies of the receiver.

Other stunning wraps are leftovers from a wallpaper roll, the remains of a roll of shelf paper, or patterned paper toweling. Paper napkins, everyday ones or with a holiday motif, can cover a small package prettily. Scraps of fabric look especially pretty on small gifts, too. Department and gift stores often provide bags with lovely abstract designs or flower patterns. These can be cut open and scissored to the needed size or used as is.

Attractive trims and ties for packages could include tail ends of knitting yarn, or maybe rickrack, seam-binding scraps, or strips of pinked material.

Children's paintings and drawings

make beautiful and unique gift wrappings. Of course children can also decorate paper with a view to using it for gift paper; applying stickers, stenciling, drawing free-hand, doing stamp art or thumbprint designs (p. 35) on tissue or shelf papers or brown bags. Children can even make "bags" by folding a piece of decorated paper in half and stapling or taping together two sides, inserting the gift contents in the remaining open side, then stapling completely shut.

Few wrappings are more eye-catching than a common brown grocery bag sporting a child's felt pen doodlings or *Patchwork Scribbles* (p. 134). Close the decorated bag with a flair. Fold down the top

opening and punch two holes. Tie with a yarn bow or, for smaller lunch-size bags, weave in a lollipop to hold it shut. This simple bag idea often proves more flexible than a box for packaging bulky or oddly shaped parts.

When you are helping two or more children make a gift for someone, use each child's talents to best advantage. The small children in the group may be too young to prepare and assemble some of the ingredients for a project, but they can do their part by creating original wrappings. This can be their special contribution to the gift giving. A child or two might prefer to design gift wraps and tags while others focus on the project at hand.

When You Do Not Want to Wrap

There are many times when you might want to add an element of surprise to an activity that you have ready for your child to do, but packaging seems too time consuming. Try this! Spread a cloth over the laid out project materials. When the project doers are standing by, remove it with a flourish, "magician style," to reveal what is underneath. What better way to

say "surprise!"

Another way to inject the spirit of mystery and fun is to let the surroundings be the wrapping. Hide the materials (if there are not too many) with written or verbal hints for finding them, treasure-hunt style. When all the parts are found, you can bet that everyone will want to do the project!

Ideas for Making and Using Directions for Activities

The suggestions for gift kits in this book include "directions" for doing the pro-

jects. If the activity is going to be done in your own home or classroom, of course you can just let the project doer use the directions right from the book. For the most part they are in simple language for the elementary school child.

When you give a gift kit to someone outside your household, simply copy the directions from the Activities section. Directions can be put on store-bought greeting cards. They can be written by hand or copied by machine right from the book and then pasted to an interesting construction paper shape, decorated bag, box, or gift sample such as a linoleum block print (p. 27). Decorate the directions with a small hint of what is to be found inside the package—patchwork pieces arranged on sewing directions or sample tiny shells for beach crafts. There are dozens of simple ways to make the card fit in with the theme of the gift kit. You will enjoy using your imagination as well as drawing on ideas from the section marked "Materials For Directions" in each activity in this book.

Children enjoy the element of suspense, so you might tuck the instructions into an envelope boldly marked MYSTERY DIRECTIONS. Directions can be fun! Add your own creative touches and let the children add theirs.

When you are writing directions to include in activity kits or to keep on file for children to use, you will need to keep in mind their ages and reading skills. For example, a child in grades one through three has a better chance of reading the instructions if you have PRINTED them. For such young children the language should be simple, in words they use every day. The challenge of reading simple directions and following them correctly can be a worthwhile learning experience for the child, if the words and writing are not frustratingly over his head.

Keep the child in mind when you are writing directions for an especially messy project involving such materials as paint or cooking supplies. The directions for these sorts of activities might be covered with clear contact paper or tape to protect them for reuse. If you use regular 3″ × 5″ file cards, maybe you have some of those "see through" recipe card jackets to use for covers.

Since many of the directions for kits in this book easily fit on 3″ × 5″ file cards, you may want to make a recipe activity box (p. 102). Each time you create kits for children, add the directions and any adaptations to this handy file for future reference. The file box could grow as you add ideas from other sources. This collection of activity directions can become a rainy day treasure trove for children or a blessing for adults who find themselves volunteering as scout leaders or school aides. The new job will not be nearly as foreboding when you can draw from familiar projects on file.

Classroom teachers might like the idea of the ongoing activity file also, listing materials along with directions so that class members can refer to it for spare-time activities or for projects that relate to specific class studies. Such a file could be indexed separately by categories such as Science, Social Studies, etc. As the selection grows, you might find it necessary to have separate activity files for each subject. Categories for a science project file might include "Dinosaurs," "Rocks," "Weather," etc. Under each heading there could be an accumulation of kit ideas which the students would enjoy assembling and doing. For the professional, parent, or volunteer this ongoing supply of project ideas can be a source drawn on from year to year.

Chapter 3

Ways to Use Activity Kits

Who Can Use Activity Kits and When

THERE ARE MANY TIMES and ways that projects can be enjoyed. Rare is the day when a child could not benefit by experimenting with new materials and experiencing new challenges. Creative activities and learning projects can be woven into day-to-day living. The right person giving a carefully chosen set of materials at the right time can accomplish this.

Parents. Parents are confronted with numerous situations in which an activity would save the day. For example, consider Dad trying to get his own project done—a mechanical job, a woodworking project, painting. The younger members of the household, intrigued, want to try. "Let me help, Dad!"

Sometimes any help from younger hands is totally out of the question for safety, skill, or other reasons. What is the solution? A few materials for a project related to Dad's activity may provide the child with something to do that will sufficiently satisfy his interest so Dad is left in peace to finish his job. Here are a few practical hints:

When Mom or Dad fixes the lawn mower, *Take Apart Kit* (p. 53) can satisfy the young mechanic. He or she can use tools and see how things are put together. The parent's problem is solved and there is a bonus! The child has enjoyed the companionship of his mom or dad, while learning something about the kind of job his parent is doing.

If the grown-up task at hand is woodworking, a project such as *Make a Table* (p. 46) or *Tape Resist Game Board* (p. 88) might leave the child happy and productive while the adult got on with the more complicated work.

Someone involved in kitchen work may find a child at his or her heels. Including a surprise cooking project or an easy recipe from this book will allow the youngster to become an involved participant instead of a frustrated observer. Imagine a preschooler using cookie cutters to shape Knox Blox (p. 109) or an older child copying mystery metric recipes (pp. 37, 80) to challenge friends or a math class.

Sitters. A baby-sitter can turn the usual evening of blood-and-thunder TV viewing into a time of getting to know the children by assembling a simple activity, absorbing for all. Mrs. Lueddeke was everyone's favorite sitter. She always came armed with a cloth bag full of intriguing things as a surprise kit—scissors and paper for cutting old-fashioned chains of paper dolls, scraps for sewing, all sorts of bits and pieces to be fashioned into something whimsical in the hours ahead. Mrs. Lueddeke's time with the children was a time of learning and sharing. A little advance planning made her job easier and certainly more fun.

Fourteen-year-old Diane, who was building a steady sitting business, took a cue from Mrs. Lueddeke. One night she appeared on the job with a sack containing corn popper and the ingredients for the popping. What a "neat" surprise! The children thought that the time spent with Diane felt like a celebration.

There are times when parents are concerned about a sitter's visit and how the time will be spent with the children. On such an occasion the parents themselves could leave a surprise kit to be opened after they have left. A simple game or craft like *Calendar Toss* (p. 121) and *Pom-Poms* (p. 33) might be good choices.

Sometimes a child is excessively apprehensive about Mom and Dad going out. Having something to look forward to might soothe the child and help him look forward to future evenings with a sitter.

Grandparents. Grandparents often hope to share their interests with grandchildren. A chat with Grandpa about his stamp collection and a gift sample or two may be fun to a degree, but a more lasting spark of interest might be struck with a hobby starter set pulled together by Grandpa. How about a box holding a stamp identification book from the post office, a pile of used envelopes with stamps to be soaked off and sorted, tweezers, and a book for storing stamps? Fifteen-year-old Craig is now an avid and sophisticated collector whose interest was sparked with just such a home-gathered kit from his grandad, seven years ago. He still remembers the time warmly shared with his elder, carefully soaking the stamps off the envelopes and matching them to pictures in the stamp identification book. The same kind of gift kit approach could encourage mutual interest in gardening, cooking, woodworking, or a whole realm of other activities.

Grandparents might have a welcome waiting for a visiting grandchild. One grandmother always had a surprise sitting on the bedpillow for her grandaughter. It might be a project to do together, but sometimes it was something to provide a quiet occupation for the youngster while Grandma took a breather! Quick kit ideas such as *Tissue Paper Stained Glass* (p. 61) or *Vegetable Sculptures* (p. 28) lend themselves perfectly to such a situation.

Friends. Children like to share their experiences just as older people do. One child will love doing a project, then packing up a set of similar materials to give to a friend, with a sample of his own handiwork included. For example, a child might have loved making his own sewing cards (p. 144). He could gather up some greeting cards, yarn, needle, and his hole punch (to loan) with a sample of one of his own completed cards and gift wrap the collection to present to a friend. The occasion might be as simple as an afternoon visit to the pal's house for some shared play, or as festive as a birthday outing in which case the punch would be a permanent gift. Five-year-old Mark gave a gift to his friend, Doug, in just this way saying enthusiastically, "This is how good times spread!"

Instead of taking a gift elsewhere, a surprise can be at your own house waiting for the arrival of guests. The children in your family might be looking forward to visitors and excitedly planning the time to be spent with them. A project or two can make the visit memorable. The activities chosen can be tailored to an afternoon visit, the extended stay of another child, or even whole families sharing time together.

The preschooler or very young members of the family will not be able to get together all of the materials to assemble a project, but they will love being part of the fun as they find certain items around the house or help during a shopping spree. They can also contribute ideas for choosing projects for various gift-giving situations and become involved in designing kit wrappings.

Group Leaders. For group leaders involved in scouts, playgroups, or Sunday School, the kit idea can mean setting up activities in an organized way to guarantee interest and orderly completion of projects with a minimum of mess. It also per-

mits appealing results achieved within the group's limited budget.

Here is a case in point. One den mother looked for an effective holiday gift idea for her scouts to make. One meeting was spent exploring the outdoors for weeds turned crisp by November cold. An ample collection was made during the outing. The next week the den mother gave each troop member a plastic bag containing a fancy bow, wooden spoon, wire, and a few of the weeds. Packaged as they were, the materials were easy to pass out in a minimum of time. From his kit materials each boy fashioned an arrangement for a kitchen wall hanging—a bow and nature's dried materials wired prettily to the spoon! The boys and their mothers were delighted with the boutique effect of the results, which had been achieved without investing in expensive hobby kits (see *Wooden Spoon Boutique Gift* (p. 96).

Teachers. Teachers continually search for new ideas to fit in with their classroom programs. They become masters at shaping creative learning activities. For them the kit idea can add a new spark of motivation for some of their project plans.

One way for a teacher to present an activity might be to have a Surprise of the Week, an activity complete with materials packaged and presented like a gift. Children look forward to a weekly surprise and eagerly watch the unveiling. Revealing the contents can be done by children on a rotating basis, as a special reward, or in recognition of a birthday or special event. Of course, the package contents would lead to a project that fitted in with the curriculum.

Some weeks the surprise might be individually bagged packages for each child. The Quick Kit sections of this book have suggestions that lend themselves to small individual gifts. They will help the teacher looking for holiday gifts to give her class or for a way to offer a new learning experience.

A teacher or leader might decide to have a Pick-a-Kit shelf or corner. A selection of boxed activity sets would be on the shelf. Periodically the collection would need to be restocked and changed. Everything for doing a project would be in a separate container—bucket, box, whatever suits best. Children could pick a box to work on as a spare-time activity or as a reward for some special contribution or job well done.

Kits might even be used for occasional awards in class. Many of the quick kits listed throughout this book would be particularly suitable for such use. For example, a simple combination of objects for a science experiment might go to the person who deserved credit as one of the class's budding scientists.

Children. For children, activity kits can become a vehicle for real social exchange. Gift giving and working on kit projects provide an avenue for creating and discovering as children cooperate and communicate with the people around them. Whether a child is simply giving a gift or participating in an activity project, he is learning the value of sharing and caring with others.

Interaction with an older person who is tuned into a child's needs can make all the difference in whether a child tries new things or not. We are all familiar with the child whose daily experience is limited to what he may gain from school and his endless hours spent immobile in front of the TV. This is a young soul who appears on the way to becoming a confirmed non-participant in life. We know, too, the children who when asked what they are planning with their friends say, "Oh, we're just going to hang around."

In contrast are the children who seem to be forever immersed in some new scheme; figuring another way to construct a building with Lego blocks while sitting before the TV set, or arranging a game with the gang in the park. Of course, personalities do differ and some children will always be more organized in their general approach to life than others, but the way in which an older person responds to a child can tip the balance. Gentle steering toward constructive activities and value placed on hours well spent can effect a change in how a child feels about himself and make a difference in his future ability to use his time well.

A child can have materials to work with, such as those in a kit project, but needs a few minutes of help or encouragement to send him on the way to being able to use them productively. Sometimes he has a scheme for some new project. Listening, and the offer of a little guidance from an older person, can determine whether or not he can gather materials and carry out his plan.

It is the parent, teacher, or older sibling who can give the word of praise and a little steering that allow a child to tackle the job that was beginning to seem a bit too difficult or accomplish the project that appeared out of reach. Children are sensitive to their interactions with the people around them. A child can blossom in the warmth of a few caring moments. Just being tuned in to what a child has on his mind will give you a clue about putting him on the road to doing an activity or implementing one of his ideas. The key is a mutual spirit of cooperation and an effort to communicate. This story is a case in point.

Andy had an idea for his ninth birthday party. He wanted a surprise party but with a new twist. He decided his *guests* should be the ones to be surprised! He had his mother call his friends' mothers to announce that the car would drive up early Saturday morning to pick up the unsuspecting guests, ready to carry them off in their pajamas or come-as-you-are attire! The destination would be his house for a "surprise" birthday breakfast.

Andy's mom was tuned in. She listened. The two cooperated in making plans. Rest assured that the birthday was a smashing success!

Another mother tuned into a "kit" activity idea. Nine-year-old Neil had a project plan he wanted to share with a friend. He loved making rockets. He knew what materials he needed for making them. It took practically no time for his mother to help him gather the necessary cardboard tubes and other items. Neil put the supplies in a bag and carried his "kit" to Mark's house where the boys spent the afternoon absorbed in rocket making.

Rockets are dangerous to set off, but Neil's dad planned a time to take the boys to the park for some exciting moments of supervised rocket firing.

In both of these cases the lines of communications were open, the boys were helped to carry out their plans, and the end result was lots of fun and a sense of accomplishment.

This same kind of cooperation will enable the children you know to enjoy planning original kit projects or doing the ones from this book. Preschoolers will share in planning, dashing about the house to find some of the needed supplies, and taking a trip to the store. They will need a helping hand on certain steps in a project. A little help and encouragement is usually all an older child will need with many project ideas. Some of the more complex undertakings will, of course, require additional supervision.

This spirit of cooperation and sharing need not always be between adult and child. It can take place between an older and younger child, or two children of the same age who can put their heads together and draw on their collective talents to encourage one another in creating and discovering.

Lots of social give-and-take can occur no matter what combination of people engage in the venture. One person can help another begin a project. Two or more may share an activity for the sheer pleasure of doing or to make a gift for someone. Creating an activity kit, enjoying a kit project, or giving a kit gift all allow children to grow amid the sheer pleasure of learning and doing with others.

Sharing Gifts and Experiences

There are a variety of ways that activity kits can be used for sharing through gift giving. Many sets of materials can be used to make a gift. Children take pride in presenting their own homemade gifts to someone else. There is pleasure in making something for a peer, for example a *Playdough Marble Roll* (p. 132). A child will also enjoy working with the members of his family in the joint making of a gift for another family. *Family Bouquet Kit* (p. 110) illustrates this kind of shared gift-giving project. (For a listing of ideas for specific gifts to make, see Appendix I in this book.)

Duplicate projects can be another means of gift giving for a child. Children like to share their experiences just as older people do. One child will love doing a project, then packing up a set of similar materials to give a friend, with a sample of his own handiwork included. For example, a child might have loved making his own *Pom-Poms* (p. 33). He could gather up some yarn, a needle, and cardboard circles and gift wrap the collection, adding a sample pom-pom for a decorative touch and concrete example of what to do with the packet contents. He will have put together the perfect present for a friend. The occasion might be as simple as spending time with a friend at his house or as festive as celebrating a birthday.

Children enjoy finding ways to share their experiences at school or with a group to which they belong. A science experiment is double fun when it can be repeated in a demonstration for others. Pride in a cooking accomplishment is multiplied when the sweets are passed out to friends.

One child spent a happy afternoon turning out bean bags wholesale. He was having an adventure with machinery—special lessons on Mother's sewing machine! When he wearied of making the bags, he spent time inventing toss games with his homemade treasures. Later he took them to school where his class used them for an arithmetic game. How important those bean bags made him feel, and what fun to see others enjoy what he had designed and made.

Families planning a festive time together can create a real lesson in sharing for any child. The occasion might be an evening get-together, a special celebration, or perhaps a weekend visit. Excited planning of the time to be spent together can include project surprises that lend to the making of a memorable experience.

One family we know gathers one day annually to observe Advent with close friends. Everyone from the youngest to the eldest in both families contribute in some way to the making and giving of holiday gifts and to the preparing of traditional foods.

Another family shares this same kind of experience, but with no particular occasion in mind. Elements of *Fireside Kit* (p. 119) have helped create this kind of time that lives in memory—everyone in a darkened room gazing at colored flames (p. 99) flickering in a fireplace, preschoolers nodding sleepily, and older children simmering down after a busy playtime and lots of pizza (p. 38).

Summer fun, a bon voyage remembrance, or a weekend visit to the home of friends in the mountains may provide happy excuses for family exchanges. *Explore Grab Bag Kit* (p. 186) gives an assortment of vacation exchanges that children can enjoy with their families.

The Child Alone

Time spent alone can be valuable to a child. Such time can offer the opportunity for learning self-reliance. A child can benefit by testing his ability to get himself started at a project and by finding how well he can do at entertaining himself constructively. He needs to learn how to concentrate on a task done by himself in a quiet, productive way. Solitary play can be a good reinforcement for the times when he must work independently in school. Following through on a project alone can give valuable practice in following directions.

Sometimes a child can gather his own materials and carry through on a project from beginning to end. Other times someone may start him off with a set of materials and some verbal or written directions.

In all but the most basic activities a very young child will need an occasional helping hand in gathering materials and working on the activity. There are exceptions. With a very simple taste activity such as *Instant S'mores* (p. 60), he can do everything. He can find the marshmallows, chocolate, and crackers and perhaps even open the chocolate container independently.

A more involved project like *Sewing Cards* (p. 144) is appealing to the preschooler, but help is needed in finding discarded greeting cards and punching holes in them. Once the materials are all together and directions for sewing given in a clear way, the youngster is on his way to a period of completely independent sewing time.

The older the child the greater his ability to be independent. He will enjoy being given the wherewithal to make something such as *Make a Table* (p. 46) which includes items that he might not be able to find without transportation. He will take equal pleasure in looking up a quick game such as *Tin Can Golf* (p. 29) and seeking out the pieces needed for play. If his mood is arts and craftsy, the materials in *Kitchen-Made Sand Art* (p. 51) or *School Photo Bookmark* (p. 101) are easily found around the house and can provide a satisfying project in which the child can manage everything completely on his own.

A ten-year-old boy's happy contribution to his class Valentine party and home celebration was heart-shaped jello treats. He looked up *Cookie Cutter Knox Blox* (p. 109). His allowance permitted him a trip to the store for the necessary gelatin and raspberry jello, and he was able to read and carry out the directions for mixing, cooking, and cutting out the hearts all by himself. His older brother crowned the project with the compliment that the shimmering hearts were "Pretty enough to hang somewhere on display!" and everyone enjoyed the tasting at partytime. The time spent working on his own had been fun and ended in further fun shared with friends and family.

KITS TO USE AT HOME

Chapter 4

Using Kits at Home

I T IS PART OF DAILY ROUTINE to fix a meal, nurse the baby, carry on a phone conversation, or turn attention to helping one of the children with a homework assignment. It is equally routine for children to become more demanding while these daily tasks are being attended to. The children wail because they are tired of waiting for dinner; the preschooler swings into naughty attention-getting action while the baby is being fed; everyone goes to pieces while Mom is on the phone; and the whole group clamors loudly for attention when one child needs desperately to understand the math assignment. These are all occasions when easy activities can contribute to a more peaceful atmosphere.

When something is needed quickly to capture a child's interest for a short period, the supplies for *Vegetable Sculptures* (p. 28) are simple to gather and have appeal for all ages. Other samples of diversions which can be hastily assembled are the game *Tin Can Golf* (p. 29) or the ex-periment with *Invisible Ink* (p. 30).

There are also many unsettling situations that do not present themselves daily but can be foreseen, like the time when a family member must have quiet for exam study, those hours that need to be devoted to preparing for weekend visitors, or the time when the baby-sitter is coming and it is quite predictable that the youngest family member will have a separation-from-mama conniption fit.

These are interludes when an already assembled project can help everything go more smoothly. A quiet, absorbing pursuit like *Kitchen-Made Sand Art* (p. 51) or *The Bag-of-Labels Make-a-Game* (p. 50) demands some extended concentration on the child's part and leaves adults free to attend their own affairs.

Another alternative, if the weather is cooperative, is the equipment for *Army-Navy Campout Pretend* (p. 45). The range of play possibilities with this kind of project is endless. It can keep children cheerfully occupied outside for hours, removed from the grownups' problems.

Impromptu celebrations are a part of life in the home. The most "scattered" member of the family leaves a room in impeccable order; he deserves recognition. A great report card is proudly displayed; a reward is called for. Small kit activities make excellent rewards. The inexpensive, hastily gathered supplies for simple activities such as *Tissue Paper Stained Glass* (p. 61) or *Ring-the-Bell Game* (p. 60) tossed into a paper bag can be a great way to say, "We're proud of you."

Unless a birthday or some equally noteworthy celebration is at hand, simplicity can be the keynote in presenting activity sets being used for home situations. There is no need for formal packaging and elaborate contents. A tray holding materials and covered with a dish towel can say "surprise" as effectively as fancy wrap. A lidded box will keep contents a secret until that special moment of "unveiling."

Materials for doing home projects can be gathered informally. The collecting of them can be made into a game to take the drudgery out of necessary household chores. When refrigerator cleaning is about to darken your day, give your spirits a lift by thinking of leftovers for a pizza-making project (p. 38) or *Vegetable Sculptures* (p. 28). Let endless toy pickup be the time when you set aside an item or two to reappear sometime later in a surprise grab bag. When a toy is not used for a while it seems brand new when it finally re-emerges.

If recycling is on your job list, remove labels from cans to go into a box for future cut-and-paste endeavors. Use newspaper pickup time for pulling out the most interesting pages for scrapbook making.

When you sort out drawers, think of the brainstorming game (p. 5) and look at old objects with new eyes. How might some of them be used for inventing new games, making fresh discoveries, or putting together something eye-catching? Put them in a special place to draw on later when an activity is needed.

What special place do you have for all this clutter? You can take a tip from the local school that has a Media Center. Clear a shelf or two, make a drawer available, or provide an area for some large boxes. This can be the place where the family gravitates to find the wherewithal for all sorts of activities. It can be the home for forgotten toys, which rediscovered offer possibilities for fresh play ideas. It can be the spot to look for materials for school reports. It becomes the place to search for something to do when there is nothing to do, and it is the workshop for creating play kits on the spot or for stashing a few carefully gathered, well-thought-out, boxed projects—perhaps one or two gleaned from this book.

When family members know there is such an activity center in the house, they will find themselves adding their own finds to the collection. That is the place where the shells can go when you arrive home from the beach. Mother's discarded jewelry can go there for later use in arts and crafts projects or to wear for a venture in dramatics or costume design.

A place to keep materials and a mind open to new ways to use them can lead you to the creation of activities that fit naturally and helpfully into your day-to-day routines.

At-Home Quick Kits

Linoleum Blocks Prints

Ages 8 and up

Materials

new linoleum block (hobby or art shop)

Speedball water-soluble ink (sold in tubes/consistency of paint)

roller

linoleum cutters (on loan)

foil pan

paper

pencil

Directions

1. Draw a simple design on the linoleum block.
2. Use the large-point cutter to remove the linoleum surface around the outside of the design.
3. With a fine-point cutter, cut detail into the design.
4. Pour ink into the pan. Run the roller through ink, then across the surface of the block. The ink will stick to the linoleum design you left on the block.
5. Press inked surface down on construction paper to print.

Vegetable Sculptures

Ages 5 and up

Materials

a variety of available vegetables such as:

carrots	parsley
zucchini	green beans
eggplant	radishes
summer squash	peppers

toothpicks

basket or box for vegetables

*kitchen knife

optional: accessories such as earrings, old eyeglass frames, hat

Directions

1. Decide which vegetable will be the main shape for your sculpture.
2. Slice and dice other vegetables for shapes to be added.
3. Stick toothpicks into the cut pieces. Stick these details on the main shape to make a face, clothes, and other decorations.
4. Use as a centerpiece or display; then cook to eat!

Pup Tent

Ages 3 and up (adult help needed)

Materials

old poncho, plastic tablecloth, or sheet

clothesline

large rocks or bricks

sketch of completed tent

Directions

1. Attach rope between 2 trees or posts at a height half the width of the cloth, poncho, or sheet.
2. Fold the cloth over the rope.
3. Pull bottom edges out as far as possible. Hold in place with 3 or 4 rocks or bricks on each side.
4. Use for a retreat from hot sun or for an overnight sleep-out.

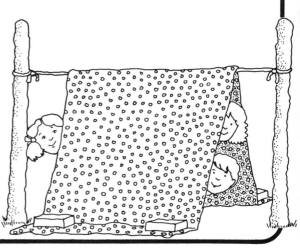

Squeeze-Bottle Squirt Play

Ages 3 and up

Materials

empty and *thoroughly washed out* dishwashing detergent bottles and/or squeeze spray bottles

Directions

1. Fill bottles with water and have a cooling squirt battle on a hot day.

Tin Can Golf

Ages 4 and up

Materials

empty tin cans

small balls (of any type) for each player

sticks or wrapping-paper tubes for clubs

Directions

1. Scatter cans around on their sides to make a golf course. Hit your balls into the cans in the fewest number of strokes. Play indoors or outside in the yard.

Nothing-to-Do Jar

Ages 7 and up

Materials

plastic jar or box

gummed label marked "Nothing-to-Do Jar"

paper scraps

scissors

pencil

Directions

1. Cut scraps of paper to fit in container.

2. Let each family member write down favorite games and activities or simple new things they would like to try.

3. From time to time pull out an idea when you want something-to-do.

4. Try a Job Jar for easy tasks to be done around the house. Try a Gift Jar for jotting down "want" or "need" ideas for gift giving.

Invisible Ink

Ages 7 and up

Materials

a lemon or small container of vinegar
paintbrush
pad of paper
150-watt bulb

Directions

1. Use lemon juice or vinegar to paint secret message on paper. Give to another "secret agent."
2. Have him hold message over the lighted 150-watt bulb and the invisible words will darken.

Weather Bureau

Ages 8 and up

Materials

inexpensive thermometer
           barometer
           rain gauge
chart or notebook
pencil
yarn
weather/cloud book from library

Directions

1. Tie yarn on flagpole or post to serve as weather vane. Position other weather-determining devices on post.
2. Check at regular times during each day such as:
   8:00 A.M. 12:00 noon 6:00 P.M.
3. Write down what you find.

Bathtub Scientist

Ages 5 and up

Materials

different size funnels
plastic tubing (sold by the foot at hardware stores)

Directions

1. Get into your tub full of water.
2. Attach funnels and tubing in varying combinations and experiment.

At-Home Activity Kits

Heavy Things Sink Kit

Experiments for tub time!

Ages 3–5

Skills
1. observation
2. experimentation
3. deductive thinking
4. making predictions

When
1. welcome to grandparents' house
2. splash gift from the baby-sitter
3. get-well gift for preschooler
4. classroom project or spare-time activity

How
1. An older child would enjoy assembling this kit for younger ones.
2. Use this tub surprise for children timid at bath time.
3. Hang the bag near the sink in classrooms and children will be tempted to experiment often.

Materials
For doing:
  Objects of different weights and materials such as:
    balsa wood
    metal spoon
    plastic cup, bowl, lid
    piece of paper
    stone
    shell
For packaging:
  onion bag
  clear contact paper or plastic sandwich bag
  string or twist 'em
For directions:
  file card

Assembling
1. Place all the test objects in the onion bag.
2. Cover the direction card with clear contact paper or plastic bag to keep dry. Tie to bag.

Directions for Heavy Things Sink Kit
1. Play this game in your sink or in your tub at bath time.
2. Examine each object. Is it heavy? Is it light?
3. Put each object in the water. Does it float? Does it sink?
4. What do you think happens to heavy things in the water? What do you think happens to light ones?
5. Experiment. Test each object. Find the answers to the questions.

Magnet Art

Make a collection! Wonderful for gift giving or game playing.

Ages 4 and up

Skills

1. imaginative use of materials
2. combining sets of objects
3. eye-hand coordination

When

1. nothing-to-do time
2. reward for a job well done
3. birthday party favors
4. group project for special occasion gifts
5. surprise for teacher

How

1. Collect magnet decorations as you clean clutter from drawers, desks, and sewing basket. Store with a supply of magnets ready to do when an impromptu activity is needed.
2. Give preschoolers a helping hand with gluing.

Materials

For making:
  magnets—circles ½″ in diameter or bars ¾″ in length (available in hobby shops, hardware, or stationery stores)
  Duco cement (white glue does not work here)
  Any or all of the following:
    pom-poms
    balls from ball fringe
    felt pieces
    buttons
    tiny pine cones
    shells up to 1″
    nickel-sized cardboard circles precut for gluing on "jewels"
    "jewels" (beads and pretty bits collected from discarded jewelry)
    optional: note pad for messages
For packaging:
  box
  ribbon
For directions:
  gift card or note pad labeled: MESSAGE
  Write directions with note at end saying,
  "Use rest of this pad for Magnetic Messages!"

Assembling

1. Tuck everything into the box and tie with a perky bow.

Directions for Magnet Art Kit

For making and using:
1. Combine materials to create original magnet designs such as: eyes on pom-poms; shells or pine cones to make funny creatures; petals on circles to make felt flowers; jewels on cardboard to make shiny baubles.

2. Use note paper to draw a picture or leave a message on the refrigerator door.
3. Mount a special collection of small shells on magnets and use a magnetic surface for display.
4. If you are a preschooler, use magnets for game playing. Experiment to see where the magnets stick—on basket, radiator. Let someone hide the magnets on magnetic surfaces. Someone else hunts to find them.
5. Play a memory game. Remove one magnet from a group on the refrigerator door while others have their eyes closed. Then let them guess which magnet is missing.

Pom-Pom Making

Each is different. Use in a variety of ways to add to the pleasure.

Ages 7 and up

Skills

1. following directions
2. observing size differences
3. color coordination

When

1. continuing project at home alone or with a small group
2. birthday gift
3. travel activity

How

1. Give with one completed pom-pom and one that has been started.
2. Keep a completely supplied pom-pom bag handy to pick up and take when you travel, enjoy while watching TV, or listening to a record.

Materials

For making:
  choice of colorful yarns rolled into balls
  large blunt-end (needlepoint) needle
  scissors
  compass (or round objects such as lids for outlining circles)
  cardboard
  pencil
  optional: felt scraps, moving eyes from hobby shops
For packaging:
  small plastic or cloth drawstring carrying bag
For directions:
  large index card with yarn border (see *Sewing Cards,* p. 144)

Assembling

1. Using compass or lids outline a pair of donut shapes on cardboard. Circles should be 2″ to 5″ in diameter; center holes should be ¾″ to 1″ in diameter.
2. Cut out the shapes.
3. Place these and other materials inside attractive bag.
4. Use piece of yarn to tie directions to the outside of the bag.
5. Decorate with a sample pom-pom tied to the package.

Directions for Pom-Pom Making Kit

For making and using:

1. Place a pair of donut-shaped cardboard circles together.
2. Using yarn lengths of about 2′, wind the yarn around the donut shape. Repeat, covering the donut evenly so the donut becomes fatter and fatter. You can alternate colors as you start a new yarn length.
3. As the center hole grows smaller, use the blunt needle to pull the yarn through. Continue winding evenly till the center hole is filled in and tight.
4. Cut yarn around outer edge of circle.
5. Separate cardboard circles slightly and tie center tightly with a piece of yarn. Remove cardboard circles.
6. Fluff up pom-pom and trim to size.
7. Use pom-poms for:
   zipper or shade pulls
   top to knitted cap
   pom-pom making gift kits
   skate or luggage identification
   bow substitutes on gift packages
   pet creature making

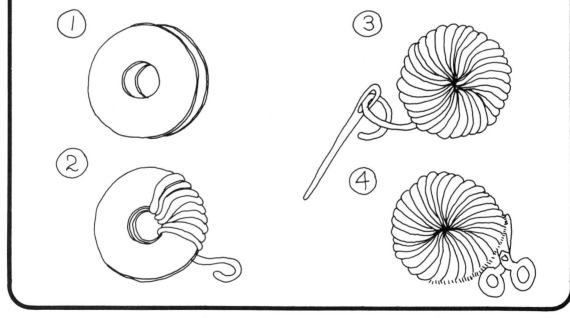

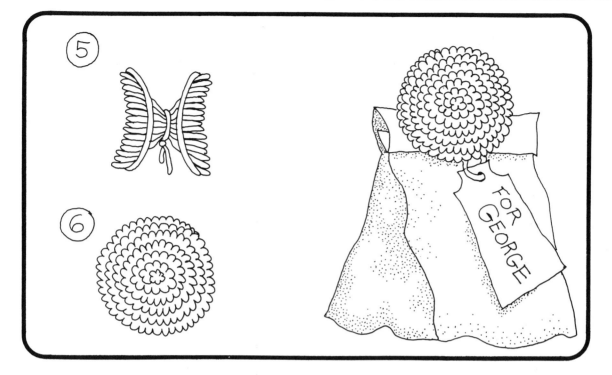

Thumb and Fingerprint Doodles

Stamp pad fun leads to fingerprint originals!

Ages 4 and up

Skills
1. stimulating the imagination
2. interpretation
3. size and shape relationships

When
1. baby-sitter's surprise
2. visit-a-friend gift
3. large group project
4. classroom spare-time activity
5. free-time activity at Day Care Center

How
1. Repeat your printing fun by duplicating materials in a kit to give a friend. Your enthusiasm and sample prints will trigger their imagination.
2. Great to give from one family to another!

Materials
For making:
   ink pad and ink (available at most stationery stores in red, blue, and black) OR
substitute ink pad:
   1. food coloring soaked into

folded paper toweling or sponge
2. watercolor or poster paint and paint brush for brushing paint on thumb or fingers

fine-point magic markers, crayons, pencil and/or pen

scrap paper or pad of inexpensive paper

optional: *The Great Thumbprint Drawing Book,* by Ed Emberley, published by Little, Brown and Co.

For packaging:

box

tissue paper decorated in fingerprint designs

For directions:

note card with thumbprint original

Assembling

1. If this is a gift for a family of children, wrap each item individually. Arrange in box.
2. Wrap box with your own thumbprint-designed paper.

Directions for Thumb-and-Fingerprint Doodles Kit

1. Press your fingertip on an ink pad and then onto the paper.
2. Thumbs are good for large areas and little fingers print well for small areas like ears.
3. Add a few pencil, crayon, or marker strokes to your print. Create your own people, animals, flowers, balloons, etc.
4. Use your favorite designs to border or decorate notepaper, invitations, gift tags, place cards, or matting for framing a picture.
5. Another idea: make a series of thumbprint designs to tell a story.

M and M Party Cookies

A metric mystery easily solved!

Ages 8 and up

Skills

1. accuracy
2. metric measurement
3. recognizing equivalents

When

1. friend-sharing time with cooking and math
2. new challenge for the best of cooks
3. metric learning for science, math, or home economics classes

How

1. Encourage children and adults to learn metrics by using metrics. The bonus for all is a batch of delicious cookies.
2. Try this as an independent, self-teaching activity for children familiar with cooking.

Materials

For making:
   metric measuring cup
   metric measuring spoons
   ingredients:
      250 milliliters shortening (Crisco) equals 1 cup shortening
      250 milliliters packed brown sugar equals 1 cup brown sugar
      125 milliliters granulated sugar equals ½ cup granulated sugar
      10 milliliters vanilla equals 2 tea-spoons vanilla
      2 eggs
      560 milliliters sifted flour equals 2¼ cups flour
      5 milliliters baking soda equals 1 teaspoon baking soda
      5 milliliters salt equals 1 teaspoon salt
      375 milliliters M and M candies equals 1½ cups M and M candies
   *mixing bowl
   *spoon
   *beater
   *cookie sheet
   *spatula
For packaging:
   plastic bags and twist 'ems
   basket or large cookie container
   wrapping and tie
For directions:
   recipe card
   blank index card and new pencil

Assembling

1. Carefully measure out each ingredient, bag separately, and label with metric amount.
2. Gift wrap new measuring spoons and metric measuring cup.
3. Include all premeasured ingredients, measuring gifts, and index card with new pencil.
4. Label recipe written in metrics with "Solve the Mystery" and use as kit gift tag.

Directions for M and M Party Cookies Kit

1. Solve the Measurement Mystery! List each ingredient on the blank card. Re-measure each bag of ingredients with cups and teaspoons. Write the amounts in metric and in cups and teaspoons by each ingredient.
2. Mix the shortening, brown sugar, and granulated sugar. Beat in vanilla and eggs thoroughly.
3. Sift together the flour, baking soda, and salt.
4. Add dry ingredients to sugar and egg mixture.
5. Stir in ⅓ of the M and M candies and save the remainder to decorate the top of each cookie.
6. Drop rounded teaspoons of cookie dough 2″ apart on ungreased cookie sheet. Decorate tops with four candies each.
7. Bake at 375° for 10 minutes until golden brown.
8. Try changing other often-used recipes to metric measurement. Start an up-to-date file box.

Easy Pizza Making

Easily assembled for the family to cook on Mom's night out!

Ages 6 and up

Skills

1. nutrition
2. responsibility in the kitchen
3. socialization

When

1. when children take over the kitchen
2. baby-sitter's surprise supper
3. meal for sick friend's family
4. birthday party supper

How

1. Allows all ages to make a meal easily according to their likes and dislikes.
2. Children can help Mom by planning this for a surprise.
3. Try pizza making for a birthday party or midnight snack.

Materials

can of tomato sauce or ground, peeled tomatoes
package of large-size Syrian bread
grated mozzarella cheese

leftovers frozen and saved:
   salami
   bacon
   pepperoni
   hamburger
   sausage
seasoning—oregano or Italian seasoning
kitchen knife (plastic variety)
*broiler pan
*can opener
For packaging:
   food-size plastic storage bag and
    twist 'em
   sandwich bags and twists
   box or brown bag
For directions:
   recipe card

Assembling

1. Precook, slice, or grate cheese and meat toppings.

2. Wrap each in separate sandwich bag and twist top closed.

3. Place Syrian bread bag and toppings in one large food bag ready for keeping in the freezer. Label "Pizza Making Kit."

4. Attach recipe to bag and give with a can or two of tomato sauce and the seasonings.

Directions for Easy Pizza Making Kit

1. Slice Syrian bread around the edge to make 2 complete bread circles. Leave on the counter for an hour to air dry or place in the oven a few minutes to dry out.

2. Spread on tomato sauce.

3. Add toppings. Place cheese on last.

4. Sprinkle on seasoning.

5. Place on cookie sheet or broiler pan under the broiler till cheese melts.

An asterisk next to an item listed in a kit's "materials" section indicates that the item is common to most homes and need not be included in the kit package.

Root Beer Making

Children feel like magicians with this experiment.

Ages 6 and up

Skills

1. following directions
2. drawing conclusions
3. experimentation

When

1. family sharing
2. two generation activity
3. scout project

How

1. Make just one bottle. Children enjoy the idea of experimenting more than drinking the finished product!
2. Grandparents can have fun starting this with young family visitors and then have ready for them to sample on the next visit.
3. Try as a discovery activity for a scout meeting. Taste test at the next meeting!

Materials

For making:

    root beer extract (purchased at a specialty food shop or at some chain grocery stores)

    small packet dry yeast

    empty quart soda bottle with screw-on cap

    *6 tablespoons sugar

    *water

    *measuring spoons

For packaging:

    brown grocery bag

    yarn tie or ribbon

For directions:

    gummed label or construction paper

    felt pen

    clear contact paper or "see through" tape

Assembling

1. Write out recipe on label or paper.
2. Stick to empty bottle and cover with clear contact paper or "see through" tape.
3. Place bottle and recipe directions in bag with other materials. Mark fragile!
4. Fold top of bag and punch two holes for yarn tie or ribbon.

Directions for Root Beer Making Kit

1. Place 6 tablespoons sugar and 1 teaspoon root beer extract into the empty quart soda bottle.
2. Fill the bottle ¾ full with lukewarm water.
3. Screw on top and shake until sugar has dissolved.
4. Add only a pinch of yeast. Too much will make the drink too fizzy.
5. Fill the bottle with cold water till it is ½″ from top. Screw cap on tightly.
6. Store root beer on its side on a tray or wrapped in a plastic bag in case of leakage.
7. Do not disturb bottle for 6 to 7 days. Root beer is then ready to sample!

Do-Your-Thing Kit

Materials ready to go allow eager children to try AT ONCE!

Ages 3 and up

Skills

1. varied, depending on the activity

When

1. for child who has a new baby at home
2. classroom or day care center spare-time activity
3. playgroup (choose and swap!)
4. birthday gift

How

1. When the new baby comes home, special moments with the first child can be spent enjoying projects from this pre-assembled gift.
2. Plan around the child's main interests and tailor the kit to his level of ability.
3. Add costumes to expand the fun of role playing.

Materials

Choose from one of these lists or spin off an idea of your own! Pick activities from the books that use materials at hand, easily available, inexpensive, discarded.

For making:

For each category choose materials from 2 to 3 activities in the book, bag each activity separately, and label with page number of the activity.

Magician

paperback book on magic, geared to the proper age level

magician's costume from the local novelty store or home-created:

top hat made from cylinder of black paper with brim cut to fit and taped on

cape cut from discarded material such as old skirt or sheet with tie-ribbon attached at neck

Scientist

book of science experiments geared to the appropriate age level

scientist's costume: lab coat made from "recycled" white shirt or blouse

Artist

arts and crafts activity book

artist's costume: smock from discarded blouse, shirt, or a work apron made from a heavy plastic bag or drop cloth. Staple or sew on neck and waist ties.

Other possible books from which to spin off a similar kit idea:

woodworking, toy making— Steven Caney's books from Workman Publishing Company

gardening—*Indoor and Outdoor Gardening for Young People,* by Cynthia and Alvin Koehler, published by Grosset and Dunlap. Add a hoe and farmer's hat for the role.

dramatic play—*Small Plays for You and a Friend* (excellent!), by Sue Alexander, published by Scholastic Book Services. Include costumes and props for one play.

For packaging:

box

wrapping

ribbon

For directions:

Cut an appropriate shape from construction paper. Example: magician's hat for magician's kit.

Assembling

1. Wrap book and activity packages individually.
2. Tuck into the box with costume and direction card. Wrap.

Directions for Do-Your-Thing Kit

1. Pick one of the prepackaged sets of materials.
2. Dress up to be the character you are playing.
3. Find the page for the activity in your new book.
4. Do the project, following the directions in the book.

Carpenter's Tool Kit

A gift that grows as the child learns new woodworking skills.

Ages 4 and up

Skills

1. manual dexterity
2. recognizing things that belong together
3. safety awareness
4. eye-hand coordination

When

1. reward for Dad's workbench assistant
2. two generation activity
3. special occasion gift

How

1. Give part of the set and then add to it on other special occasions.
2. Use real tools so children are not frustrated by what flimsy toy tool sets refuse to do. Supervise the very young child and share his pleasure with him.
3. What a super gift from an adult who enjoys woodworking.

Materials

For doing:
Give from one or more of these groupings.

Set 1:
  hammer—large-headed claw hammer

nails—galvanized roofing nails have large heads
foam packaging materials (hardware store will save these for you) and/or soft wood scraps (check lumber store discard barrels)
optional: carpenter's apron for holding nails—homemade version or advertising give-away at building supply stores

Set 2:
  saw—hacksaw that takes 10″ to 12″ blade (14 to 18 teeth per inch)
C-clamp
  scraps of soft wood (pine) or corrugated cardboard or foam packaging
sandpaper

Set 3:
  file—10″ combination shoe rasp is good
  scraps of soft wood

Set 4:
  screwdriver—short, stubby one; Phillip's head; or one 6″ to 8″ long with ¼″ blade
  screws— Phillip's head ones for Phillip's head driver
nails
  optional: eggbeater type hand drill
For packaging:
  optional: bought or homemade tool box OR
  sandwich bags and twist 'ems

cardboard box
brown paper wrapping
ribbon
For directions:
   3″ × 5″ cards

Assembling

1. Put small supplies such as screws and nails into sandwich bags, twist shut, then place all materials and directions into proper sized box or tool box.
2. Wrap.

Directions for Carpenter's Tool Kit

For doing:
   If you are a beginner or a child between 4 to 7, use these directions.

hammer and nails

1. Hold nail between forefinger and thumb of left hand and place it on the foam or wood. With right hand tap, tap gently with hammer. The nail will drive easily into the foam packaging with only a few hits. Once you've developed good aim in hitting the nail, try the same process on wood.
2. Once the nail is sticking into the wood, move your left hand away and whack harder until the nail goes in as far as you wish.

file

1. Clamp wood into C-clamp or vise if you have one. Hold firmly if you don't.
2. Run file across wood in sawing motion. See how much sawdust you can make! See how much wood you can wear away!

sawing

1. Clamp wood or cardboard or foam into C-clamp.
2. Saw back and forth gently. See how far you can go through the wood!
3. Smooth sawed edges with sandpaper.

screwing

1. Nail a little hole into the wood or make a hole with a drill.
2. Screw screw into hole. Practice more screwing.

For older children give directions and, perhaps, materials for one or more of the following:
   Make a Table Kit (p. 46)
   Napkin Holder Kit (p. 87)
   Log Bird Feeder (p. 86)

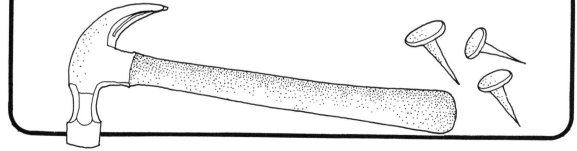

Army-Navy Campout Pretend Kit

Enter the world of let's pretend through the doors of an Army-Navy store!

Ages 3 and up

Skills

1. role playing
2. imagination
3. language arts

When

1. when children come to play
2. birthday or holiday gift
3. costume party

How

1. "Add to" this gift kit. As special occasions arise or a reward is needed, a new item can be added to the Army-Navy collection.

Materials

For making:

Make a selection of appealing items from an Army-Navy surplus store. The following kinds of items are often available at excellent prices and are far more substantial than the simulated items available at toy stores:

canteen
belt
tent
mess kit
backpack
insignias (to sew on shirt)
first-aid kit
child-size uniforms
medals and ribbons
various kits and containers to hang on belt

Fill out with things around the house such as:

bedspread or sheet "tent" camouflaged in a tie dye project
metal Band-Aid box taped to belt as first-aid kit
homemade medals

For packaging:

sturdy box for permanent storage
optional: contact or wallpaper with patriotic motif
glue or tape

For directions:

construction paper
marker

Assembling

1. Cover the box with patriotic paper.
2. On construction paper, write "Army-Navy Pretend Kit" in large letters with directions beneath. Tape or glue onto box.

Directions for Army-Navy Camp-out Pretend Kit

1. Pretend you are camping out on assignment. Use everything in this box, and use things you can borrow from home or invent yourself.
2. Try these starting ideas for play with the kit:

    Camp in your fort (tree, tent, box)

    Sail your ship (sandbox, wading pool)

    Bail out of your plane (swing) and rescue someone

    Eat chow back at camp (picnic time!)

Make a Table Kit

Results *impressive* and useful! Simple to do!

Ages 6 and up

Skills

1. concentration
2. following directions
3. hammering and screwing

When

1. to do when grown-ups are involved in workshop work
2. special occasion, birthday
3. scout or small group project

How

1. Collect materials in advance ready for the right moment to do.
2. Try this super, quick activity with a young child whose interfering enthusiasm is slowing down a larger project that adults are working on. A few minutes spent doing this will satisfy the youngster's desire to make or fix something and leave him with a game table to play on while the grown-ups continue their project.

Materials

For making:

formica-topped piece cut out in making the opening for sink or vanity (home improvement centers, lumber dealers, kitchen or bathroom specialists, or builders are good sources for these scrap pieces)

matching large pails—about 5-gallon capacity:

empty driveway sealer drum

house paint can

detergent pail

jelly pail from bakery (45-lb. capacity)

2 to 3 large-headed common nails

3/16″ diameter

10¾″ × 10″ pan head tapping screws with 3/16″ flat washers

*hammer

*pliers

*screwdriver

pencil

optional: tape to cover unfinished table edge

For packaging:

regular size plastic food storage bag

twist 'em

large trash bag

ribbon

For directions:

construction paper

tape

felt pen

optional: game—forgotten, inherited, or from a garage sale!

Assembling

1. Remove any handle from pails with pliers.
2. Place pencil, nails, screws into plastic bag and twist shut.
3. Write directions on paper. Optional: tape to cover of game box.
4. Put all materials into trash bag and ribbon-tie shut with directions.

Directions for Make a Table Kit

1. Turn pails upside down. Use hammer and nail to drive 4 to 5 holes into the bottom of each pail, about 1½″ from edge at even intervals around the pail.

2. Place board, formica side down, onto floor. Set pails in the middle of the board. Pail bottoms with nail holes will be right on the board.
3. Make a pencil mark through each of the holes. Remove pails.
4. Use hammer and a nail to make a shallow hole where each pencil mark is. These holes will be your screw holes.
5. Place pails with holes over the holes in the board. Put washer over a hole. Take a screw and put it through the washer and press firmly (into the board beneath). Begin to screw with your fingers. Finish the job with the screwdriver.
6. Repeat with the remaining washers and screws.
7. Now you have a super game table. Put tape roads on it and run little cars on them. Do a clay modeling project on it. Play a card game with a friend or try the new gift game. Then turn it upside down and use the pails for a toss game with balls, bean bags, pennies etc!

Masking Tape Floor Games Kit

Bring outdoor games inside! Work off steam with lots of games at bargain prices.

Ages 4 and up

Skills

1. balancing
2. strengthening large muscles
3. physical coordination
4. competition

When

1. company is coming
2. housebound by weather
3. party entertainment
4. day care activity

How

1. Preschoolers need help handling great lengths of tape and placing them correctly.
2. Masking tape applied to carpet or floor is easily removed.

Materials

For making:
roll of masking tape
*scissors
game accessories:
    Net Volley or Basketball use one or all of the following:
        nerf ball
        bean bag
        finger pop-its
        plastic lid frisbees
        scrunched-up paper ball

Hockey:
    empty wrapping tubes for sticks
    plastic lids for pucks
Hopscotch: pebble or bottle cap
For packaging:
    box or drawstring sack
For directions:
    separate piece of oaktag or file card with a game diagram on one side and directions written on the back.

Assembling

1. Box or bag the playing accessories, tape, and directions for one or more games.

Directions for Masking Tape Floor Games Kit

For making:

Net Volley (2 or more players)

1. Choose room where small objects can be moved to make play space.
2. Place tape in straight line across room to divide it evenly.
3. Equal or unequal numbers of players stand on each side of the line "net" and volley play equipment.

Basketball (1 or more players)

1. Make a short tape line on floor.
2. Place laundry or wastebasket on a chair or table some distance across the line.
3. Shoot baskets from behind the tape-line using Nerf, bean bag, etc.

Hockey (2 or more players)

1. Use tape to outline your rink on the floor. Mark off the two end goals.
2. Use empty wrapping tubes as hockey sticks and plastic lids for pucks.
3. See who scores 10 points first by keeping the lid in motion while trying to score through the opposite goal.

Hopscotch (any number of players)

1. Use tape to make standard playing grid, then play away with a pebble or bottle cap.

Bag-of-Labels Make-a-Game Kit

Reading magic for the beginner or nonreader!

Ages 3 and up

Skills
1. reading readiness
2. perceptual matching
3. memory

When
1. family game time
2. small group project
3. when sick
4. shopping with Mom

How
1. Preschoolers will like the Help Mom Game!
2. One child will like to complete a game set, ready-made with game directions, to give a friend. The two can share the playing.
3. Each child in a group or class glues one or more pairs. Put the cards together and, presto, you have a deck!

Materials
For making:
    30 or more 5″ × 7″ index cards
    bag of canned food labels (2 matching labels for each product)
    glue
    *scissors
    rubber band or box for cards

For packaging:
    brown paper bag
    yarn tie
For directions:
    index card decorated with a label or picture of product

Assembling
1. Remove labels from a wide variety of canned products that you use often.
2. Make a sample pair of cards.
3. Tie the sample cards and remaining blank cards with a rubber band, or place in box.
4. Bag all materials with directions for making cards and directions for one or more games. Tie shut.

Directions for Bag-of-Labels Make-a-Game Kit
For making:
1. Make cards like the sample pair in the kit.
2. Cut label to fit on card. Brand name and contents must show—"Campbell's Chicken Noodle Soup"
3. Glue label to card.
4. Make another card to match.
5. Repeat till you have 15 or more pairs.

For games:

Help Mom Game
1. Mom will pull out the label cards

that match some items on her shopping list. Take them to the store in a bag or purse.

2. Help fill Mom's cart. Look for containers that match the cards as you go up and down the aisles. Check with Mom to see how many of each item she wants.

Memory Game (1 or more players)

1. Take your complete set of cards and mix them so pairs are not together.
2. Put all the cards, one by one, facedown on a table or rug.
3. Take turns with your partner turning over two cards each time. If the labels match, you keep the pair. If they do not match, you return them to the same spot, facedown.
4. The winner is the player with the greatest number of pairs.

Go Shop (like card game Go Fish, 2 players)

1. Mix up cards so pairs are not together.
2. Deal out 7 cards to each player. Put other cards in pile facedown. Watch out! Don't let anyone see your cards!
3. Ask the other player for a label you need to make a pair. If he has it, he must hand it over. If not, he will say "Go Shop" and you draw a card from the pile. Now it is his turn.
4. When you get a matching pair, put it down in front of you. The winner of the game is the one with the most pairs when all the cards have been played.

Kitchen-Made Sand Art

Sand art without the sand.

Ages 5 and up

Skills

1. following directions
2. designing patterns
3. fine motor control

When

1. I-don't-know-what-to-do project
2. a gift to take and do with a friend
3. playgroup, scout, or other group project

How

1. Older children will try layered hill and valley effects. Preschoolers will simply layer colors evenly.
2. Older children are better able to mix the colored sugar and prepare the kit for a friend.

Materials

For doing:

    food coloring

    3–4 small dishes

    granulated sugar—enough to fill the jar of your choice

        To color sugar: Divide sugar into dishes. Leave one batch white. Put a few drops of different color food coloring into each of the others. Mix thoroughly. Allow to dry before packaging.

    wide-mouthed jar with lid (baby food, jelly, or peanut butter)

    spoon

For packaging:

    plastic sandwich bags

    twist 'ems

    box

    wrapping

    ribbon

For directions:

    colored paper

Assembling

1. Package sugar in separate sandwich bags and twist 'em.
2. Pack sugar, spoon, and jar into box with directions.
3. Gift wrap.

Directions for Kitchen-Made Sand Art Kit

1. Pour sugar into small dishes.
2. Spoon a layer of colored sugar into the jar.
3. With the tip of the spoon, poke dents in the sugar in several places right next to the glass.
4. Spoon in another layer of sugar in another color.
5. Make some little sugar hills in several places next to the glass. You will see designs beginning to grow!
6. Make more layers and dents and hills to fill the jar, and complete the design.
7. Put on lid to finish.

Take Apart Kit

Imagine being TOLD to take something APART!

Ages 4 and up

Skills

1. small motor coordination
2. eye-hand coordination
3. seeing relationships
4. manipulation

When

1. for younger folk when Mom or Dad are engaged in an important no-touch fix-it project
2. bad-weather-day activity
3. great birthday gift!
4. continuing activity for classroom enrichment corner

How

1. Older members of the family can keep a discard box to stash cast-off items. Take Apart fun can then be produced instantly when needed.
2. Keep in mind the age of the child, what the parts of the item are, and safety factors when choosing an item to dismantle.

Materials

For undoing:
  a selection of tools such as screwdriver, pliers, or tool kit (can be a "loan")
  Any one of these from your own discard pile, garage sale, or car

junk yard:
  alarm clock
  stove timer clock
  watch
  mechanical adding machine
  car radio set
  typewriter
  camera
  telephone
  record player

small appliances (PLUGS AND WIRES REMOVED):
  toaster
  blender
  portable mixer

optional: Collection of pipes and joints offers endless connecting and disconnecting possibilities. These are available from a local plumber.
duco cement
scrap of wood or cardboard
Fixed By Camel, Sweet Pickles Series by Reinach and Hefter, published by Holt-Rinehart Winston. A comical book for "fix it" children to enjoy.
For packaging:
  box or heavy brown paper bag
  newspaper wrapping would hint at a "work" project inside!
For directions:
  piece of brown cardboard

Assembling

1. Wrap tool kit or tools separately.
2. Place tools, take-apart object, optional materials, and directions in box.
3. Wrap or tie everything into a paper bag. Label "Take Apart Kit."

Directions for Take Apart Kit

1. Use the tools to take this object apart.
2. Once it is apart see if you can fit some of the pieces back together.
3. Save some of the smaller pieces that have interesting shapes such as nuts, gears, etc. Nail, glue, or screw them to a piece of wood or cardboard to make an interesting design.

KITS TO USE
IN A GROUP

Chapter Five

Using Kits in a Group

WHETHER YOU ARE A TEACHER, volunteer group leader, or parent, there are bound to be occasions when you find yourself gazing into the eyes of more than one expectant child. A teacher must manage overall plans for her class, provide for free moments, and devise ways for coping with the unexpected. The playgroup parent or scout leader needs to look ahead to be ready with activities for each meeting and to be prepared with strategies for short periods when everyone is getting restless. Parents find themselves embroiled in plans for sleep-overs, birthday parties, or the sudden unexpected demands of "the gang" appearing after school.

Whether your group is large or small your key to success lies in being prepared. You will need ideas for the more involved group projects as well as a trick or two tucked up your sleeve, ready in a twinkling when the unforeseen is tossed your way. Having several sets of materials all ready and designed will put you in a position to manage the children successfully and happily.

Being prepared leaves *you* in the driver's seat. It means you will not be dashing about for last-minute supplies while the children veer completely out of control or lose interest just as you finally find yourself ready to begin.

Having more than one activity available for a single block of time can contribute to the productivity of the children. Variety at your fingertips gives you flexibility. It enables you to shift gears to adapt to the mood and immediate needs of your group. What if your normally low-keyed youngsters appear in a fever of jittery excitement? A quiet activity requiring intense concentration like *Quilt Making Iron-On Kit* (p. 72) can be put aside in favor of a more noisy, physical pursuit such as *Olympic Games Kit* (p. 90).

The kind of project you choose should

take into account the individual characteristics of the children—ages, skills, abilities, and interests. In choosing a kit idea from this book or in shaping your own ideas, make your final selections based on what you know about Dawn's ability to cut, Susan's attention span, Jonal's interest in science, etc.

For example, your group may be woodworking enthusiasts. You might plan on making the *Napkin Holder* (p. 87). Package the required project materials along with paints, stains, and brushes from the workbench. The children can bring their own hammers. One child may take the whole time to finish his holder. Another might finish early and launch into embellishing his work with decorative touches of paint. Another fast worker does not enjoy painting so he uses some extra wood scraps and nails for additional fun with hammering. You will have successfully allowed for the varying abilities and interests in your group.

There are various ways for a group as a whole to share an activity. You could choose a project which allows each to do essentially the same thing at the same time, or a project which provides for the group dividing up tasks in working toward a common goal. For example, scouts can plan for the next week's project by picking an idea and dividing the responsibility for bringing needed materials. They can all begin work on the project together at the next meeting. Another idea would be for a child to extend an invitation to friends for an afternoon cooking spree and have everyone bring an ingredient . . . a perfect chance for using a cooking activity idea from this book. Try *Best Ever Cocoa Mix* (p. 67). The guests measure and mix. Copies of the recipe are made and a sample container filled to accompany each child

home. Once clean-up is over, the testing of the mix will take care of refreshment time!

"Fill-in" times require different planning. "Fill-in" times can be those spare minutes before school or when group members are still arriving and individuals within the group need settling down. They are those times when some people have finished the main project and are casting around for new worlds to conquer. They are the blank times when an appealing activity can entice a rowdy in the group to constructive pursuits.

"Fill-in" activities are best when geared for one or two children to do alone. They are the same sorts of activities that also serve well during TV watching or nothing-to-do times at home. Once understood, they need no special direction and can be picked up or put down any time. Often they can be self-taught.

Examples might include *Pom-Pom Making* (p. 33), a birdwatching identification game (p. 149), matching postmarked envelopes to a U.S. or world map (p. 132), or opening a combination lock with math clues (p. 171). A photo album (p. 132) to which people could add clippings, photos, or poems at any convenient time would be fun.

You can put these hints for your group planning to use if you *know* you have a group coming, but what if your child brings home his restless gang looking for instant fun? There is certainly no time to organize an elaborate project or shop for missing ingredients. A gang of kids are ready and waiting!

One new material or one simple idea can do the trick. A roll of masking tape is common to most homes and combined with scissors and floor space can initiate group efforts for designing a floor game (p. 48), floor map for house and truck play, balancing contests, or word building. Once the group has exhausted the fun with these ideas they are apt to create their own ideas and extend the play possible with one roll of tape even longer.

Simple spur-of-the-moment ideas from the Quick Kit sections can also be a help in organizing unplanned fun. Try an impromptu party letting the children design party hats, placemats and games all from scraps, or turn them into good deed elves and direct their efforts and energies to raking or shoveling for a neighbor in need.

Group situations both planned and unplanned are regular occurrences for parents with children. Take advantage of the collection of talents available and the "group spirit" to produce simple and productive fun that includes everyone.

Quick Kits for Groups

Ring-the-Bell Game

Ages 3 and up

Materials

bell (larger size easier for younger
children to hit)
ball (Nerf for inside play)
rope or string

Directions

1. Attach bell to one end of the rope or
string.
2. Hang from tree branch or indoor
pipe.
3. Throw the ball and try to ring the
bell.
4. See how far away you can stand and
still hit the bell.

Instant S'mores

Ages 3 and up

Materials

Hershey's *fudge* sauce or other *thick*
chocolate sauce or ready-made
chocolate frosting
tiny marshmallows
graham crackers

paper napkins
plastic knives
*can opener

Directions

1. Use plastic knives or butter spread-
ers to frost crackers with chocolate.
2. Sprinkle with a few marshmallows.
3. Munch!

Scene Building Blocks

Ages 4 and up

Materials

large wood scraps (from lumberyard
or new construction site)
sandpaper
markers

Directions

1. Sand edges well.
2. Use markers to draw special scenes
such as jungle, harbor, or Army.
3. Check your toy box for trucks, animals, soldiers, and other miniatures
to use with your new blocks.

Tissue Paper Stained Glass

Ages 7 and up

Materials

2 pieces construction paper
colorful tissue paper scraps
white glue
*pointed scissors

Directions

1. Cut two identical simple shapes from construction paper, e.g., a bell or butterfly.
2. Holding the shapes on top of one another, cut non-connecting open spaces inside the shape.
3. Separate the shapes. The cut designs will match.
4. Glue tissue paper scraps over the spaces on one shape; then glue second shape over the tissue paper layer to give a finished stained glass look.
5. Hang in a window.

Actress Pretend Kit

Ages 3 and up

Materials

any combination of these:
- jewelry
- sunglasses
- evening shoes
- scarves
- ballet slippers
- glamorous cast-offs such as:
    - night gown
    - peignoir
    - formal dress
    - cocktail dress
    - ballet costume
- makeup
- sample perfume bottles or discarded ones filled with water to pick up scent

Directions

1. Act the part of your favorite TV star.
2. Add new props to your costume kit.

Whittling Fuzz Sticks

Ages 8 and up

Materials

jackknife, new or loaned
medium-sized dry branches
experienced adult!

Directions

1. Hold stick securely and whittle away from yourself. Whittle pieces of bark just enough so they peel down but remain attached to the stick.
2. Makes great kindling for your next fire!

Bird Nest Building Bag

Ages 3 and up

Materials

mesh onion bag

string

assortment of materials such as:

    colored yarn

    tattered baby blanket string

    unraveled rope

    material scraps

optional: library book, *Jane's Blanket,* by Arthur Miller, published by Viking Press, New York.

Directions

1. Stuff the bag with colorful scraps.
2. Use string to tie shut and attach to a tree branch in the spring.
3. Wait a few days; then look around your yard for nests made with familiar scraps.

Pond Adventure Kit

Ages 5 and up

Materials

fine gauge net

plastic container for collecting

identification book, e.g., *Pond Life,* published by Golden Books, or *In Ponds and Streams,* by M. Waring Buck, published by Abingdon Press.

Directions

1. Scoop up plants and creatures in net.
2. Place in container and observe.
3. Find pictures of your plants and creatures in the book. Read about your discoveries.
4. What larger plants and animals did you see? Use the book to find out about them, too.

Mystery Smelling Jars

Ages 4 and up

Materials

blindfold

baby food jars containing an assortment of strong-smelling foods such as:

vinegar

mustard

Worcestershire sauce

strawberry jam

catsup

chocolate sauce

Directions

1. Cover your eyes with your hands (preschoolers) or put on a blindfold (older children).
2. Have someone hold an uncovered jar under your nose. Guess what is in it.
3. Try this with all the jars.
4. Make some more smelling jars.

Weigh Things Kit

Ages 6 and up

Materials

inexpensive set of scales from drugstore, dimestore, or hardware store

objects to weigh, such as:

bolt

pencil

dollhouse furniture

toy car

coin

optional: paper and pencil

Directions

1. Weigh two objects. Write down the weight. Take away one of the objects. Make a note of what the remaining object weighs.
2. Compare weights as you add or take away objects. Write down your findings.

Mini Carpenter Kit

Ages 4 and up

Materials

large supply of wood scraps or foam packaging material (hardware and appliance stores will save packing for you)

nails of different sizes, U staples, and corrugated fasteners, (roofing nails best for preschoolers)

felt pen

*hammer

Directions

1. Nail wood scraps or foam pieces together to make an interesting design or object.
2. Add details with felt pens.

Instant Wall Hanging

Ages 3 and up

Materials

strip of heavy masking tape (12″ × 2″ is good)

waxed paper (press tape to this for easy giving)

some of these:

sand

tiny pebbles

dried materials from nature

tiny shells

Directions

1. Peel tape from waxed paper. Lay it sticky side up.
2. Arrange materials on the surface in a pretty design.
3. Tack or hang for display.

Activity Kits for Groups

Fingerpaint Fun Kit

Slippery fun for the fingertips! Lots of squeezing and shaking, too.

Ages 3 and up

Skills
1. artistic expression
2. experimentation
3. manipulation

When
1. playgroup
2. special occasion gift, birthday or holiday
3. activity gift for staying overnight with a friend
4. kitchen activity while Mom works

How
1. A child would love to assemble this kit to do with a friend.
2. For the preschooler's first tries at mixing and moving paint a formica surface is perfect! Later, when the focus is on design more than feel, a child may prefer to preserve his efforts on paper.

Materials
For doing:
  powdered tempera paint, one color to fill shaker
  shaker (powdered sugar shaker or container such as empty baking-powder tin with holes punched in the top)
  small plastic squirt bottle (plastic honey, mustard, or catsup server, or empty hand lotion bottle)
  liquid starch to fill squirt bottle
  sponge
  optional: roll of shelf-lining paper
    old shirt personalized with iron-on tape for paint smock tape
For packaging:
  basket, box, pail, or plastic shoe box
  ribbon or ready-made bow
For directions:
  greeting card or colored paper dressed up with fingerpaint decoration

Assembling
1. Arrange materials in basket, pail, or box with directions.
2. Tie with ribbon or decorate with bow.

Directions for Fingerpaint Fun Kit
1. Squeeze a glob of liquid starch onto a formica table surface or onto a piece of shelf paper. If you use shelf paper, tape it onto your work surface to keep it from slipping.
2. Shake some powdered paint onto the starch.

3. Mix the paint and starch with your fingers. Slide it around the work surface with your fingertips, the sides of your hands, or even your arm. Enjoy the feel!

4. Shake in more paint for darker color if you wish.

5. Make designs: dots, lines, crosses, swirls.
   Make pictures and hand prints.

6. Use your hands when you need to erase.

7. Use the sponge for wiping up.

8. Extra! Preschoolers take special note! Another time try using shaving cream on a formica surface. Make designs, erase, make more till the cream vanishes! Fun for *everyone*.

Best Ever Cocoa Making Kit

Delight in measuring and sampling!

Ages 4 and up

Skills
1. reading directions
2. measuring
3. organization

When
1. a family holiday gift project (see *Fireside Kit* p.119)
2. a skating or sledding party
3. after-school treat
4. bad weather, indoor activity

How
1. Allow preschoolers to stir the mixture, decorate, and fill cans.
2. When this is done with a small group of friends, minimize the expense by having each child bring an ingredient.

Materials
For making:
    11-ounce jar Cremora

10⅔ cups powdered milk
1 pound Nestle's Quik cocoa
½ to 1 pound confectioners' sugar
airtight containers: empty coffee tins, large Crisco cans, etc. (one recipe fills 4 one-pound coffee tins ⅔ full)
optional for decorating containers: burlap contact paper, material scraps, or wallpaper remnants
optional: glue
*large mixing bowl
*large spoon
For packaging:
    large plastic food bag
    twist 'em
    grocery bag
    yarn tie
For directions:
    recipe cards

Assembling

1. Premeasure powdered milk and twist closed in plastic bag.
2. Precut material to cover cans.
3. Place powdered milk, other ingredients, cans, decorating materials, and some blank recipe cards into the grocery bag.
4. Fold bag at top and punch 2 holes. Secure yarn through holes.
5. Write mix recipe and kit directions onto recipe cards. Attach them to yarn tie on bag.
6. Label bag BEST EVER COCOA MAKING KIT!

Directions for Best Ever Cocoa Making Kit

1. Decorate cans by covering with material.
2. In a bowl mix together powdered milk, instant cocoa, Cremora. Add ½ to 1 box of the confectioners' sugar—according to taste.
3. Spoon mix into cans.
4. Write mixing directions onto recipe cards and attach the cards to the can lids.
   Mixing directions:
   1. Fill mug ½ to ¾ full with cocoa mix.
   2. Add boiling water or very hot tap water. Stir.

Narcissus Planting Kit

Ages 4 and up

Skills
1. plant science
2. seeing relationships
3. observation

When
1. Sunday School, daycare
2. scout, playgroup
3. party favor
4. special occasion gift

How
1. Let children plant a bulb as a party activity and take the "favor" home with directions for care.
2. Do as a family contest and plant one bulb for each family member. Measure growth regularly. Watch to see which blooms first and which grows best.

Materials
For doing:
  narcissus bulb
  plain or colored pebbles, vermiculite or perlite—enough to fill a margarine tub (sources: garden shop, driveway, building supply house)
  small margarine tub
  optional: tiny sea shells
For packaging:
  2 plastic sandwich bags
  larger bag, plastic, or paper
  ribbon or string

For directions:
  colored paper or card decorated with flower sticker, drawing, or cutout from seed catalog, a narcissus plant if possible!

Assembling
1. Tie pebbles and narcissus bulb into separate sandwich bags.
2. Tie all materials into larger bag with directions attached to outside.

Directions for Narcissus Planting Kit
1. Fill tub with pebbles, vermiculite, or perlite.
2. Plant bulb in the pebbles so pointed end is up and about ½ of the bulb is showing. Sprinkle tiny shells over surface of pebbles for a pretty look!
3. Add water till it touches the bottom of the bulb.
4. Put in a dark place 2 to 3 weeks till plant begins to sprout. Skip this step if your bulb has a sprout when you plant it. Keep watered.
5. Place in sunny spot. When flowers appear, move to a less sunny spot.
6. Keep and enjoy or give your plant to someone special, like Granddad on his birthday or a teacher on Valentine's Day.

Big-Mouth Disguise Kit

Be "swallowed up" in the fun of this creation!

Ages 6 and up

Skills

1. verbal expression (monster interpretation)
2. originality
3. imagination
4. small motor control

When

1. playgroup parade
2. to express feelings about monsters
3. small group puppet production
4. costume party

How

1. Use inexpensive art supplies because the sturdiest of monster boxes are short-lived.
2. Grown-ups cut jagged mouth lines and pop-up eyes—too tough for kids!
3. Color Big Mouth green for St. Patrick's Day. A fearsome leprechaun!

Materials

For making:

sturdy box with solid sides, about as deep as from top of child's head to waist

decorating materials:

colored tape

yarn, old mop or paper to fringe for hair

colorful scraps of fabric, colored paper, contact paper (for eyes, brows, etc.)

poster paint in a variety of colors including white for teeth or finish off cans of leftover paint or spray paint

large paint brush

glue

newspaper

paint smock or shirt (loan)

optional: *Where the Wild Ones Are,* by Maurice Sendak, published by Harper and Row (buy paperback or borrow from library)

*large, sharp knife

*scissors

For packaging:

the Big Mouth box

plastic bags

twist 'ems

large ribbon

optional: photo of a Big Mouth that another child has already created and enjoyed.

For directions:

homemade card with child's drawing of a fearsome monster!

Assembling

1. Use large sharp knife to cut a mouth with jagged teeth along the middle of three sides of the box at the front edge.
2. Cut 2 large half circles on top of the

box at the front edge.

3. Bag art materials. Tuck them into the Big Mouth box.

4. Tie ribbon around Big Mouth so the mouth stays closed and art supplies stay in!

5. Attach directions with ribbon.

Directions for Big-Mouth Disguise Kit

1. If you have the book *Where the Wild Ones Are,* look at it for some monster ideas or to get you in the mood.

2. Make a wide mouth line around the teeth with colored tape, fabric, or paper strips or with paint.

3. Paint your box as you imagine your monster. Use polka dots, stripes, your favorite color, or even a calico design!

4. Lift up eyes cut in top of box.

5. Add hair, eyes, ears, and nose with scrap materials.

6. Treasure hunt your desk and drawer for accessories to add special personality to your Big Mouth —maybe a blown balloon nose, wire glasses frames, or a silly hat to balance on his head!

7. Pop Big Mouth over your head. Like a jack-in-the-box let your face appear inside the mouth.

8. Pretend you are a life-sized puppet and give your own Muppet show with your Big Mouth-making friends.

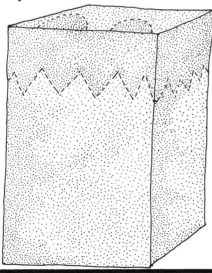

Quilt Making Iron-On Crayon Kit

Absorbing fun with crayons and fabric scraps creates a work of art!

Ages 6 and up

Skills

1. original drawing
2. planning a pattern
3. measuring

When

1. scout group
2. rainy day vacation project
3. sick child
4. moving away gift
5. new baby gift

How

1. Give this as a surprise project for a group to do. The members share the creating and end up with a lasting gift to give a friend or to use as a church school or classroom hanging. Make the squares more special by adding the names of group members.
2. Members of a family each make a square. Cover a pillow with the pieces as a keepsake or as a remembrance for grandparents.
3. A sick child will love to make a coverlet for teddy bear or baby doll.
4. Grandmother and grandchildren will love time spent together—designing, shopping, and sewing.

Materials

For making:

box of fabric crayons (from dime-stores and hobby shops)

precut squares of old sheet or other *synthetic,* white fabric, about 6″ × 6″ (4 for a preschooler, more for older children or group project) OR

an entire *polyester* sheet for large wall hanging, tablecloth, or group project

precut shelf-paper squares, same size and number as fabric squares (or estimate enough to cover sheet)

enough material to border and back quilt (gingham is attractive and easy to measure and cut)

interlining (enough to cover backs of squares or sheet—you will need to estimate)

straight pins

needles, sewing, and embroidery thread

embroidery floss or yarn

ruler

optional: colorful seam binding tape, enough to border each square optional: pictures of quilts for ideas (check women's magazines and craft catalogs)

*sewing machine

*iron

For packaging:

gift box

gift wrapping

For directions:

plain notepaper with picture of quilt or snipping of fabric glued on in patchwork design

Assembling

1. Precut squares of fabric and paper.
2. Wrap materials individually if this kit is for a group project.
   Each child can unwrap a part of the surprise.
3. Arrange materials in gift box with pictures for simple quilt designs. Tuck in directions, too.
4. Gift wrap outer box.

Directions for Quilt-Making Iron-On Crayon Kit

You'll end up with a super wall hanging or coverlet!

1. Plan the theme for your quilt pictures. Some theme ideas: town landmarks for a friend moving away, a nature theme (birds, flowers, animals), "my/our favorite things," abstract designs, family memories.
2. With fabric crayons, color a design or picture onto each paper square. Color dark for clear bright trans-

fers. Simple drawings are best. If words or names are used, they must be written in reverse! A mirror will help you.

3. Place and pin each paper picture square facedown on a fabric square or on the whole sheet.
4. Pad the ironing board with newspaper. Place the sheeting down flat on the padded ironing board. Heat the iron to cotton setting. Iron firmly and evenly—not too fast—over an entire paper square to transfer the design. You can tell when the transfer process is complete because the colors will show through on the paper. Transfer all the designs to the fabric in this manner.
5. You are ready to sew your quilt!
   For individual squares:
   a. Lay out quilt squares on flat surface. Pin, baste, and machine stitch together.
   b. Pin and sew to interlining and material backing.
   c. Tie corners of square with embroidery floss.
   For entire sheet quilt:
   a. Pin, baste, and machine stitch seam binding to border squares OR
      Use ruler and crayons to draw a cross-stitch border around each design. Do the cross-stitching in yarn or embroidery floss.
   b. Pin and sew to interlining and material backing.

Mystery Feely Box Kit

Things around the house make a perfect touch and feel game!

Ages 3–8

Skills

1. stimulating the sense of touch
2. description
3. identification

When

1. playgroup
2. classroom game
3. party game
4. sick in bed

How

1. An adult or older child can make the feeling box.
2. Younger children love suggesting and collecting touchables or scraps that feel good to add to the box.

Materials

For making:
  sturdy cardboard box with top
  large cloth or paper bag
  common items to guess by feel (feather, orange, straw, etc.)
  scraps of materials in many colors and textures (sandpaper, carpeting, cotton balls, fabric, etc.)
  glue
  optional: textured contact paper cut into letter shapes to spell child's name on the box
  *scissors

For packaging:
  bag for scraps
  gift wrap
For directions:
  stiff paper or large file card made "feely," too, by gluing on 2 to 3 small scraps of different textures (sandpaper, onion bag, yarn, etc.)

Assembling

1. In top of box cut circle large enough for child's arm.
2. Cut bottom out of bag and insert into circle cut from box.
3. Put a few "feely" items into the box.
4. Glue directions to box. Label box "MYSTERY FEELY BOX."
5. Put glue, scraps, and optional letters into scrap bag.
6. Gift wrap feeling box and scrap bag together.

Directions for Mystery Feely Box Kit

1. Put your hand into the box. Feel and guess what is in there.
2. Add other items to the box. Let your family and friends add mystery items to the box.
3. Cut out pieces of material and glue them to the surface of the box. Stick on your name if you have contact paper letters.
4. Feel! Is it rough or smooth, hard or soft, bumpy, slippery, scratchy? What else?
5. Talk about the objects you feel inside the box and what they feel like.

Follow the Footsteps Kit

A chance to make up your own game rules!

Ages 3–7

Skills
1. noticing likenesses and differences
2. observing logical sequence
3. movement exploration

When
1. playgroup
2. party activity
3. remedial tutoring
4. rainy day

How
1. Use lots of space—a room, two rooms, or all through the house!
2. Use your own ideas to vary the directions and game rules.

Materials
For making:
   construction paper or brown paper
      bags
   chalk
   optional: "balancing" book
For packaging:
   brown bag
   yarn tie or ribbon

For directions:
   giant footprint cut from construction paper

Assembling

1. Cut out giant footprints, larger than foot size of the largest child playing.
2. Place all materials in brown bag. Fold top and punch two holes.
3. Thread yarn tie or ribbon through the punched holes and tie bow.
4. Write directions on a footprint and attach to outside of bag.

Directions for Follow the Footsteps Kit

1. Toss the paper footprints down on the floor in a crooked line.
2. Take little steps and giant steps trying to reach each footprint. Keep hands and feet from touching the floor in between.

3. Make up rules like:
   Follow the numbers in sequence.
   Make a word as you step.
   Spell your name or the name of a friend.
   Use the footprints to make a treasure hunt trail.
   Use the chalk to mark letters and numbers for your made-up games.
4. Extra! Balance a book on your head as you count, spell, and step on the footprints. Walk backward.

Rhythm Art Kit

Like finding pictures in the clouds!

Ages 5 and up

Skills
1. spontaneous creative expression
2. listening
3. perception
4. imagination

When
1. whole family share activity
2. classroom
3. friend visits and shares project
4. TV substitute on bad-weather day

How
1. Consider the small motor skill of the preschooler who might be doing this. If he can manage a coloring book page passably, he can do this, but this is *far* more creative.
2. Try giving this to several children in one family. It appeals to all ages, so brothers and sisters can have fun doing it together!

Materials
For doing:
    charcoal (from art stores or hobby shops)
    several large pieces of paper (newsprint is fine) or large pad
    poster paint (powdered paint is cheapest and is available at hobby shops. Mix in jars with lids.)
    "kindergarten" brushes (large easel brushes with long handles)
    empty container (for rinse water)
    record with smooth, catchy rhythm (loan or gift)
    optional: tape
For packaging:
    sandwich bag
    box
    large plastic bag (to cover all if the drawing paper cannot be put flat in the box)
    big stick-on bow
    rubber band
    tape
For directions:
    bright paper decorated with cutout or drawing of musical staff and notes

Assembling
1. Roll up sheets of paper and secure with rubber band.
2. Put charcoal in sandwich bag.
3. Arrange all materials in the box. Label box RHYTHM ART KIT. If you must stand paper pad or roll upright, use a large plastic bag to cover all.
4. Stick on bow, and tape on directions.

Directions for Rhythm Art Kit

1. Fill container with rinse water. Spread out some newspaper on the working surface and set out paint, water, charcoal, and brushes. You may want to tape the drawing paper to the work surface in a few places so it will not slide.
2. Play the record and listen to the music for a while. Move your writing hand and arm in rhythm to the music.
3. With charcoal, make lines on the paper in rhythm to the music.
4. Look carefully at the "squiggly" lines you have made. Do you see a picture in the lines? This is like finding pictures in the clouds!
5. With charcoal, darken the outline of the picture that you see.
6. Paint it. Paint over any lines you do not want in your picture. Remember to use the rinse water when you change paint colors.

Strumming Kit

Fun with sound on a strange strumming instrument!

Ages 6 and up

Skills

1. sensorimotor development
2. rhythm
3. learning to differentiate sounds

When

1. campfire singing
2. rhythm band
3. school music project
4. fill a nothing-to-do time

How

1. Make one for yourself and your friends will want one, too.

Materials

For making:
  large can (2-pound coffee can)
  yardstick
  nail
  thin wire
  masking tape
  *hammer
  *hand drill

For packaging:
  shopping bag with handles
  ribbon

For directions:
  construction paper
  glue

Assembling

1. Write directions on construction paper and glue to outside of bag.
2. Collect all materials for making and put in the bag.
3. Tie handles together with ribbon. Label "STRUMMING KIT."

Directions for Strumming Kit

1. Place open end of can down and hammer nail in center of closed top.
2. Drill a hole in the yardstick about 6″ from one end.
3. Tape the yardstick to the outside of the can.
4. Tie a large knot on one end of the wire and thread unknotted end through the hole in the can. Be sure the knot holds inside the can when the wire is pulled taut. If it does not, thread the wire through a cardboard scrap and then through the hole in the can to assure a firm grip.

5. Bend the yardstick slightly and thread the second end of the wire through the yardstick hole and wrap around the yardstick to hold in a bow position.
6. Experiment with different strumming sounds as you bend the bow more and more, then less and less, while plucking the wire.

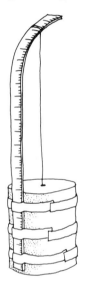

Metric Snack Kit

A metric delight! Not inexpensive, but delicious and nutritional!

**Ages 3–7 can shape treats,
8-year-olds and up can do whole project**

Skills

1. metric measurement
2. making comparisons
3. independence in the kitchen (no cooking needed)

When

1. do with a visiting friend
2. home help on mastering metrics
3. bonus activity for school math group

How

1. Assemble this kit to do with a single child learning about metrics or give as a challenging activity for 2 to 3 children to make as a group project.
2. Younger children feeling left out on this project can join in on the shaping of the balls and rolling in powdered sugar.

Materials

For making:
   ingredients to purchase:
   8-ounce package dates
   8-ounce package figs
   2¾-ounce package almonds
   11-ounce package of the *medium* -size dried apricots
   3 ounces wheat germ
   8 teaspoons honey
   optional: powdered sugar
   metric measuring cup
   metric measuring spoons
   *food grinder
   *bowl
   *mixing spoon
For packaging:
   grocery bag or produce basket
   pinked material strip for ribbon tie
   inexpensive metric conversion chart
      for gift tag
For directions:
   index recipe card

Assembling

1. Write recipe on card including required ingredients and amounts to purchase.
2. Decorate the back of the metric chart as a gift tag.
3. Place recipe and all ingredients into bag or basket.
4. Tie ribbon and attach gift tag.

Directions for Metric Snack Treat Kit

1. Use metric measuring cups to measure and the food grinder to grind the *following in order:*
   78 grams almonds (2¾ ounces or all of purchased bag)
   113 grams dates (4 ounces or ½ of purchased box)
   76 grams figs (2⅔ ounces or ⅓ of purchased package).
   Combine in a bowl with the following:
   84 grams wheat germ (3 ounces)
   40 milliliters honey (8 teaspoons).
2. Mix well. Form into small balls and roll in powdered sugar. Recipe makes approximately 2 dozen balls.
3. Cap each ball with a dried apricot.
4. Now feast!

Pringle's Bug Catcher Kit

Fun to make and fun to tote on a bug catching expedition!

Ages 8 and up

Skills

1. reading and following directions
2. identification
3. associating things that belong together

When

1. small group activity; scouts, campers
2. family camping trip
3. backyard explorations
4. classroom science project

How

1. A nature-loving adult can share outdoor discoveries with a young friend by giving this Bug Catcher, ready-to-make or ready-made.
2. Family members can share the making of this kit before a woodsy outing.
3. This is a dandy home for tiny toads and other small creatures, too!

Materials

For making:
   Pringle's can or breadcrumb can with plastic lid
   fiberglass or wire screening
   paper
   *paper punch
   *pointed scissors
   12″ string
   *exacto or kitchen knife
For packaging:
   paper or plastic drawstring bag
   ribbon
For directions:
   file card and/or bright-colored paper cut in shape of ladybug or butterfly

Assembling

1. For preschoolers precut window openings. (see directions)
2. Copy directions on card or colored paper cutout.
3. Tuck materials into bag.
4. Use ribbon to tie directions onto bag. Punch holes if necessary.

An asterisk next to an item listed in a kit's "materials" section indicates that the item is common to most homes and need not be included in the kit package.

Directions for Pringle's Bug Catcher Kit

1. Use knife to cut large window openings on two sides of the can. For sturdy results, do *not* cut holes exactly opposite one another.

2. Use scissors to cut screen. Use the paper liner from the Pringle's can as your pattern.

3. Roll screen into tube shape and slip into the container.

4. Use paper punch or scissor points to punch two holes on opposite sides of the can near the top.

5. Thread string through the holes and knot the ends for a handle.

6. Use paper punch or scissor points to make holes in the lid. Put lid on can top.

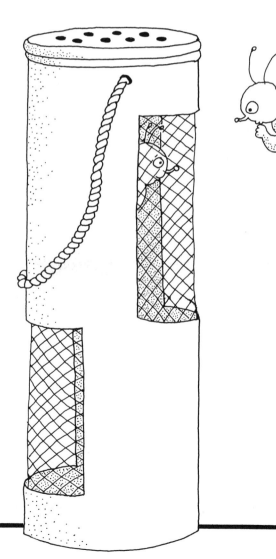

Clothesline Story and Display Kit

An entertaining way for children to tell a story or practice a variety of skills

Ages 5 and up

Skills
1. storytelling
2. strengthening left-right progression
3. grouping in logical sequence

When
1. playgroup
2. classroom display
3. at home sick

How
1. Encourage practice and review of different skills.
2. Children love to arrange and rearrange displays on a line.

Materials
For making:
    clothesline or sturdy string
    clothespins, pinch type
    several 8½″ × 11″ sheets construction paper or newsprint
    crayons
    felt pen
    magazines of interest to child receiving gift
    glue
    *scissors
For packaging:
    box

    gift wrapping
For directions:
    colored paper

Assembling
1. Place materials in box and wrap.
2. Write or Xerox directions on colored paper.
3. With clothespin, pin directions to ribbon on gift box.

Directions for Clothesline Story and Display Kit

1. Hang your clothesline where it is easily reached and seen. Try to place the line in a spot where it can stay for a few days.
2. Think up a simple story (an old favorite or one you make up). Illustrate your story with drawings or magazine clippings.
3. Hang your pages in order to tell the story. Start at the left end of the clothesline and work to the right.
4. For fun, scramble the story pages. Let a friend try to put them back in order.

Other things to do:

1. Pin up number facts or spelling words that you need to practice.
2. Take a vacation from writing and reading. Hang up a sheet on your clothesline and enjoy an indoor fort. (See *Pup Tent* pp. 28)
3. Have a spur-of-the-moment art show. Invite friends to bring their own art work and come for juice and cookies. Hang up the creations for everyone to enjoy.
4. Write words on separate sheets of paper. Hang them in alphabetical order.

Log Bird Feeder Kit

The fun continues long after the making!

Ages 3 and up

Skills
1. increasing attention span
2. eye-hand coordination
3. observation

When
1. scout, playgroup, Sunday School project
2. two-generation sharing
3. getting well

How
1. Use this with *Bird Watching Kit* (pp. 149).
2. Use this kit as a cold weather project; then enjoy winter birdwatching with the family.
3. Make this as a gift to give a favorite senior citizen.

Materials
For making:
   1″ to 2″ diameter log cut to fireplace length
   nails with large heads (roofing nails)
   lots of plastic caps from gallon milk containers
   large screw eye
   wire or string
   plastic knife
   peanut butter

optional: to mix with peanut butter:
   birdseed, breadcrumbs, oatmeal, cornmeal.
For packaging:
   colorful yarn or ribbon
   food-size plastic bag
   margarine tub with lid
For directions:
   card with bird picture—homemade if you like!

Assembling
1. Scoop some peanut butter into the margarine tub, mixing in optional ingredients.
2. For a preschooler premake the feeder (see directions). Leave peanut butter filling, log hanging, and bird watching to do.
3. Drop tub, nails, screw eye, wire or string, bottle caps, and plastic knife into plastic bag (just tub and knife for preschooler).
4. Tie yarn or ribbon around the log. Attach plastic bag and directions.

Directions for Log Bird Feeder Kit

1. Nail bottle caps all over the log. Top of caps should be next to the log.
2. Using nail, hammer shallow hole into one end of log. Screw screw eye into hole for hanging.
3. Use plastic knife to fill caps with peanut butter mixture.
4. Hang from tree branch that you can see from a window.
5. Watch for bird visitors.

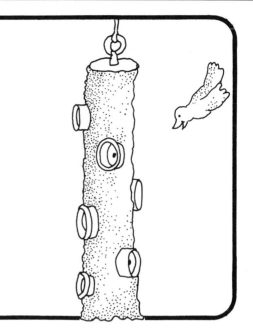

Napkin Holder Kit

A few simple steps and presto!—a handy household item!

Ages 6 and up

Skills

1. accuracy
2. measurement
3. eye-hand coordination

When

1. scouts or other small group
2. to do when adult woodworking makes a child want to try some, too
3. Mother's birthday, teacher gift, or house gift

How

1. Very successful when prepackaged for each child in a group.

Materials

For making:

¾" × 8" × 8" piece of particle board or soft wood

½" × 1" × 6" wood strip

2 3½"–4" *common* nails with large heads (toss in spares for bending disasters!)

2 ¼" or ½" screw eyes

optional: spray paint or paint with brush

napkins, special-occasion ones if this is a holiday or birthday gift

*pencil

*hammer

For packaging:

regular-size clear plastic food storage bag

twist 'em or ribbon
For directions:
    file card

Assembling

1. Put all materials into plastic bag and tie.
2. Attach directions to ribbon.

Directions for Napkin Holder Kit

1. Use hammer and small nail to make shallow hole in center of each end of wood strip.
2. Screw the screw eyes into the holes.
3. Place the wood strip in center of 8″ × 8″ board; then make pencil marks on the board through the centers of the screw eyes.
4. Place nail in center of a screw eye right on the pencil mark. Hammer it in partway. It will stand up like a tall peg, about 2¾″ high.
5. Put the other nail through the other screw eye the same way. The wood strip will slide up and down the nails easily.
6. Tuck napkins into the holder.
7. For extra fun, paint or stain the holder. Write "NAPKINS" on the wood strip with magic marker, paint, stencils, or stick-on letters. Decorate with designs.

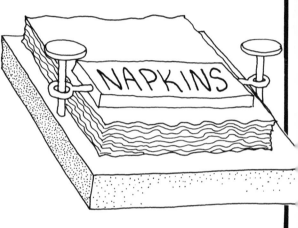

Tape Resist Game Board Kit

Make your own tic-tac-toe and other games!

**Ages 4–7 (help make and able to play)
8 and up (whole project)**

Skills

1. inventive designs
2. organization
3. manual dexterity

When

1. group projects—scout, playgroup
2. joint family project
3. time shared with a friend
4. activity for a confined child

How

1. Copy a trail game like Chutes and Ladders. Create a theme like skiing

or mountain climbing.

2. Enjoy as a cooperative family gift-making project. One member designs; one tapes; one paints.

3. Give each group member a package of materials. Let each design his own game or abstract pattern to keep or give.

Materials

For making:

wood scrap suitable to game being made (8″ × 8″ good for tic-tac-toe)

masking tape

game playing pieces: nickels and pennies, soda-pop caps, milk caps

sandpaper

spray paint or stain

paint brush

newspaper

For packaging:

onion bag, heavy plastic bag, or drawstring sack stitched from scrap material

For directions:

file card or colored paper

Assembling

1. Put all materials into bag and tie shut with directions attached to outside.

Directions for Tape Resist Game Board Kit

1. Spread newspaper over your work surface.

2. Sand edges of your wood scrap till smooth.

3. Tape to make tic-tac-toe, other game, or abstract design on board. Be sure edges of tape are tightly sealed so the paint line will be smooth.

4. Paint, spray, or stain entire board. Dry.

5. Peel off tape. Take out bottle caps or other game playing pieces. PLAY!

Olympic Games Kit

Test physical skills with the simplest equipment!

Ages 3–11

Skills

1. eye-hand coordination
2. large motor control
3. competition

When

1. small group activity
2. birthday party event
3. playing with a friend

How

1. Use indoors or outdoors.
2. The youngest child can assemble these easy-to-gather materials to make kits to do with another child or group of children.

Materials

For making:

  2–3 straws
  poker chip, 50¢ piece, hockey puck, lid, or other disk-shaped object
  2–3 paper plates
  marshmallows
  string
  needle
  tape or chalk
  sticks or wrapping-paper tubes (safest for preschoolers)

For packaging:

  plastic sandwich bag
  regular-size plastic food bag
  ribbon

For directions:

  paper with sports picture glued on for decoration

Assembling

1. Use needle and string to prethread marshmallows individually.
2. Put marshmallows into sandwich bag. Put this and all other materials into larger bag and tie shut with ribbon.
3. Write directions on back of sports-decorated paper and attach ribbon.

Directions for Olympic Games Kit

1. Make starting and finishing lines with tape, string, or chalk.
2. Hang marshmallows from ceiling (indoor pipes) or tree branch.

Then: HAVE OLYMPIC GAMES!

Javelin Throw: Toss straws. See who can throw farthest.

Discus Throw: Throw paper plates. See who can throw farthest.

50 Yard Dash: Push disk with stick or paper tube. See who gets to the finish line first!

High Jump: Jump to bite hanging marshmallow.

KITS FOR SPECIAL OCCASIONS

Chapter 6

Using Kits for Special Occasions

W<small>E ALL LOOK FORWARD</small> to celebrating the customary holidays with old traditions and new ideas in decorating, cooking, and gift exchanging. Teachers in the classroom and adults at home are in a mutual fever of preparations with children at these times. Largest on the calendar loom the winter holidays, but many of the gift and activity ideas used for this season lend themselves to other occasions throughout the year. Creative projects offer endless opportunities to prepare for special events and for making gifts. They can be the means of expressing praise, appreciation, or understanding of the things happening in the lives of people who are important to us.

Treats from the kitchen are a traditional part of every celebration. One fam-

ily enjoyed baking, then dressing up their delcious creations in gift wrappings. This enthusiasm was channeled into producing fancy wrapped Christmas presents for the neighbors. Dad's birthday also served as a time for testing their culinary talents. Each child made a different batch of cookies, decorated their own tins, and tucked them in the freezer for Dad's lunches. Their gifts from the kitchen were a happy solution to gift giving on occasions throughout the year.

Craft or other activity ideas that lend themselves to making presents like *Sparkling Window Shade Pulls* (p. 146) or *Wooden Spoon Boutique Gift* (p. 96) may be just the thing for children to try in anticipation of gift-giving occasions. The end product of many kit projects may be appropriate for teacher's bridal shower, aunt and uncle's housewarming, or one of those calendar occasions like Mother's Day or Valentine's.

Maybe you or your children want to give a gift that will immerse the recipient in an engaging project. A child who had just been presented with a new baby brother or sister would welcome such a gift. A set of materials for doing *Paper Doll Set Design Kit* (p. 147) or *Miniature Scene Kit* (p. 140) are perfect ways to show a child that he is remembered. It also gives him something with which to occupy himself when his parents must devote their attention to baby.

There are many other times when the project-type gift helps both adults and children. For example, a sick parent will welcome a demand-free rest when his child is given a gift set of materials for doing a quiet project.

On some occasions you will want an activity kit that contains the ingredients for creating a celebration. Look at *Party Kit* (p. 120) or *Fireside Kit* (p. 119) for some ideas. Cooking projects can provide appealing refreshments for a festive occasion. *Instant S'mores Kit* (p. 60) or *Pizza Making Kit* (p. 38), for example, make irresistible party treats for children. Arts and crafts kits can produce decorations to festoon a party table, to deck a room, or to improvise engaging party favors. One ingenious grandmother created a prebirthday activity for her ten-year-old granddaughter who was home sick with the flu. It was the *Cloth Flowers Kit* (p. 138). Grandma gave a helping hand to start the work. The end result of this project, which was so absorbing for the confined child, was an attractive table decoration for the upcoming birthday party.

Homemade party favors can be success-

fully made from kits as can party games. One way of presenting a game kit is to package the playing materials in bags tied with bows. At playing time, older children can untie the bag and set up the game as part of the festivities. Younger children's games should be set up ahead of time. Playing pieces needed for the games—dice, pennies, foam pop-its, balloons, etc.—can be tied into small bags for each player.

Dramatic and costume ideas presented "kit" fashion lend themselves to the children's most favorite of holiday celebrations—Halloween! You might use the costume ideas from this book, or you and an older child could pull together some things you have on hand for your preschooler's Halloween costume box. If you are a teacher or playgroup mother, add a few bits to the group's costume corner so the children will have fresh possibilities for costume design activity. Using home kit costuming is much more fun *and* much less expensive than using standardized, commercially purchased costumes. See *Big-Mouth Disguise* (p. 70) for a costume idea that is adaptable to the making of many different characters.

A few odd materials tucked into a box marked "costume" can set a child's imagination spinning. Wiring circuits and a cardboard box sent 12-year-old Ken into action designing an imaginative "talking" robot for Halloween that still has the neighborhood shaking its collective head in wonderment.

The gift of a special service can be used to mark a calendar celebration or to say, "I care." *Lighten-Your-Load Help Kit* (p. 122) is an example which can be adapted to a time when the children around you want to surprise someone with a "helping hand" gift. Materials for the chosen job can be cleverly packaged with tickets attached to announce the purpose of the gift. In some cases the giver will need to arrange a convenient time for delivery of his services. This kind of giving means a personal contact that is not possible with a standard sort of gift selection.

As daily events unfold we often create our own special occasions responding to momentous and not so momentous happenings in the lives of the people around us. Use kits for acknowledging the more impromptu but all-important events that are part of our lives: the accomplishment of a child who at last pulls up a consistently low grade; Dad's announcement of a promotion, a milestone event in the life of the whole family; little sister's big catch on her first fishing trip. The sharing of gifts and celebration can figure in all of these situations, and activity ideas can be adapted to them.

Sometimes an ordinary day can be turned into a celebration to make people feel important and cared for—a beribboned treat from the kitchen and a homemade card with a message, "We raked your leaves," or, "We shoveled your driveway," could make the homecoming of vacationing neighbors or grandparents special indeed. Use your own creativity to see how you and the children around you can make a special occasion out of an ordinary sort of occurrence.

Friends want to acknowledge all kinds of happenings in one another's lives. Everyone—child or adult—experiences the terror attending a trip to the hospital. An excited child going off to camp for the first time deals with mixed feelings of pleasure and apprehension. Confusions of happy anticipation and fear of the unknown are experienced by the people making a major move. Mother and Dad leave on a much needed vacation. The children left behind feel uncertain about this sudden abandonment. All of these are times when a gift or some special attention can soothe the affected individuals and show that someone does care.

Many important occurrences just do not call for happy celebrations. Perhaps a long awaited trip is canceled. A something-to-do surprise might provide a mind-distracting consolation. A family you know well may experience a period of overwhelming worry or the loss of a loved one. A gift given or a service offered can lend support in such a troubled time. *Family Bouquet Kit* (p. 110) or *Lighten-Your-Load Help Kit* (p. 122) are ways to show your concern for the other family.

Special occasions dot our day-to-day living in dozens of ways. Giving and using of activity ideas can be woven into the fabric of daily happenings to celebrate happy events and to acknowledge more sober moments. The value of simple projects is not just in the materials and doing, but in the sharing of experiences and showing of concern for others.

*An asterisk next to an item listed in a kit's "materials" section indicates that the item is common to most homes and need not be included in the kit package.

Quick Kits for Special Occasions

Bag of Clay

Ages 3 and up

Materials

bag of clay (bought or homemade)
Best Clay Recipe:
1. In one bowl, mix 3 cups flour, 1½ cups salt, 6 teaspoons cream of tartar.
2. In a second bowl, mix 3 cups water, food coloring, 3 Tablespoons cooking oil.
3. Combine the two mixtures in a saucepan. Cook over low heat till thick, stirring constantly.
4. Cool. Knead well. Keep refrigerated.

recipe card with directions for making Best Clay
2–3 cookie cutters
toy or full-sized rolling pin

Directions

1. Set up your materials on formica counter or table.
2. Use rolling pin, cutters, and fingers to make wonderful clay shapes.
3. Keep homemade clay in airtight container in fridge when not in use. Make more when you need it.

Wooden Spoon Boutique Gift

Ages 6 and up

Materials

wooden spoon
premade bow
dried weeds, plucked in autumn
florist wire
optional: paint or stain with brush

Directions

1. Stain or paint spoon if you wish.
2. Wire an arrangement of dried materials onto the wooden spoon.
3. Wire on bow. Use enough wire so there is a tag end to twist into a loop for hanging.

May Day Pin Basket

Ages 7 and up

Materials

2" × 1¼" miniature party favor basket (card and hobby shops)

1½' of ¼" grosgrain ribbon

small chunk plastic foam or cotton puffs to fill basket

colorful fabric scrap, large enough to wrap over foam or cotton

white glue

pins and needles (pins with colored, round heads are pretty)

*scissors

Directions

1. Cut piece of ribbon to fit over length of handle. Cut another to fit around the top edge of the basket.
2. Squeeze glue onto basket edge and handle. Press on ribbon.
3. Use leftover ribbon to make bow. Glue bow onto side of basket.
4. Wrap foam in fabric. Stick into basket so fabric looks smooth on top.
5. Stick in pins and needles.

Jelly Bean Taste Test

Ages 3 and up

Materials

bag of *fruit-flavored* and licorice jelly beans, or gumdrops

Directions

1. Close your eyes tightly.
2. Pop a jelly bean (or gumdrop) in your mouth.
3. Guess what the COLOR of the candy is by tasting the sweet!

Ice-Cream-Cone Clowns

Ages 3 and up

Materials

box of ice-cream cones

quart of favorite ice cream

assortment of trims, bagged: jimmies, chocolate bits, cherries, gumdrops, etc.

paper baking cups

ice-cream scoop

Directions

1. Place paper baking cup "collar" upside down on plate.
2. Scoop ice cream onto cone. Place upside down on paper.
3. Use trims to make hair, eyes, and other parts of face.

Heidi's Paper Bag Piñata

Ages 5 and up

Materials

large grocery bag

tempera paint in several colors

paint brush

streamers (bought crepe paper or hand-cut tissue paper)

rope

scotch tape

stuffing materials: party favors, candy, newspaper

plastic bat

blindfold

*scissors

Directions

1. Stuff the bag with newspaper, candy, party favors. Tie shut.
2. With paint brush drizzle paint over the bag in colorful design.
3. Tape streamers to the top.
4. Use rope to hang piñata over a tree branch or basketball hoop.
5. Let someone raise and lower the piñata while the blindfolded player swings at the moving piñata with a plastic bat.
6. Let each player take turns till the piñata breaks open and candies and favors fall to the ground.
7. Scramble for treats!

Flame Color Mix

Ages 6 and up

Materials

Any or all:

 1 cup salt for yellow color flame

 1 cup borax for green color flame

 1 cup calcium chloride for orange color flame

Directions

1. Mix the chemicals.
2. Sprinkle on fireplace logs. For extra fun drill holes in a log and fill the holes with the chemicals.
3. Enjoy the color when the logs are lit.

Party Favor Bag

Materials

 brown paper lunch bag filled with favors, folded at the top, two holes punched in fold with pretty ribbon or yarn threaded through and tied, child's name marked colorfully on bag

 ping pong ball (split a package)

 2 to 3 straws (split a package of novelty straws if you find them)

 colored chalk, fat chunks if possible (split a package)

 paper with directions for use of chalk, ball, straw (carbon copies for more than one)

 optional: gum, candy, and trinkets

Directions

Game 1: Play with 1 or more other kids.

1. With chalk draw 2 lines several feet apart. Mark one line "start," the other "finish."
2. Put balls on the "start" line. At the signal "go" blow through your straw to make the ball roll. Blow it to the "finish" line. First one to finish is the winner.

Game 2: Play this one alone.

1. Mark a trail with your chalk. Use the straw to blow the ball along the trail.
2. Make up your own blow, toss, or other kinds of games using the chalk, ball, and straw.

Speedy Birthday Cake

5 and up

Materials

packaged cake mix which includes pan and frosting, the kind that allows mixing, baking, and frosting in the same pan

small tube of cake-decorating frosting for writing

birthday candles

2 to 3 toothpicks

Directions

1. Follow the mix directions for mixing, baking, and frosting cake.
2. Use toothpick to draw words and design on top of cake. If you make a mistake, erase it by smoothing the frosting with a knife.
3. Squeeze decorating frosting over the lines you have drawn.
4. Add candles and celebrate!

Violet-by-Mail Surprise

Ages 7 and up

Materials

strong African violet leaf with 1½″ stem

plastic wrap

tape

envelope

light cardboard

Directions:

(Avoid mailing in bitter cold.)

1. Wrap the leaf flat in a piece of plastic wrap. Seal with tape.
2. Cut a piece of cardboard to fit envelope. On it write directions for growing violet:

"On arrival, place leaf in a glass of water. After roots grow, fill a pot with soil and plant."

3. Tuck cardboard with directions into the envelope. Add wrapped leaf. Send to someone special.

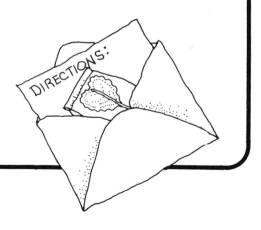

Mystery Purse

Ages 8 and up

Materials

old pocketbook filled with items such as:

    tickets (theater, parking, sports)

    snacks (gum, beef jerky, raisins)

    train, bus, subway schedules

    makeup

    paperback

    real coins

    maps

    lists

    eye-catching, unusual items that help build a picture of the purse owner

Directions

1. Examine the purse contents.
2. What do you think the owner of this purse is like? Take turns telling something about this person.

School Photo Bookmark

Ages 4 and up

Materials

small school photo

thin cardboard, oaktag, or heavy paper cut 8½″ × 2½″

business envelope

clear contact paper or wide clear tape

white glue

stickers (chosen to fit the occasion or holiday)

marker

Directions

1. Glue photo to cardboard strip.
2. Use marker and stickers to decorate strip with designs that fit the occasion for giving. Sign your name.
3. Cover entire strip with clear contact or tape.
4. Pop this bookmark into the envelope and send to someone special!

Activity Kits for Special Occasions

Activity or Recipe Box Kit

Make a collection of activities or recipes.

Ages 8 and up

Skills
1. writing
2. reading
3. organization
4. varied activity skills

When
1. A teen or grown-up will enjoy giving this kit to a child, then adding new activity or recipe cards from time to time.
2. The giver can decorate the recipe box himself. The gift kit might then include the finished box, recipe, or activity cards and the wherewithal to do a project from one of the cards.

Materials
For making:
  plain recipe box, metal or wooden
  starter selection of recipes or activities:
    easy-to-do ones for young children,
    variety of ideas that adapt to different situations
  magazines and mail order catalogs to cut and paste
  colored index cards or pretty recipe cards
  index dividers
  white glue for wood box, cement for metal box
  clear spray or Deft with brush
For packaging:
  box
  gift wrapping
For directions:
  one of the recipe or index cards

Assembling
1. Box all materials and wrap prettily.

Directions for Activity or Recipe Box Kit
1. Cut designs and pictures from magazines to decorate the box.
2. Glue clippings on box, rounding paper over the corners to fit. Dry.
3. Spray or finish with Deft when dry.
4. Collect some recipes or activities to add to your card file.

Collage Memories Kit

A background of memories for a favorite photo.

Ages 6 and up

Skills
1. montage-collage technique
2. cutting and pasting
3. categorization

When
1. family exchange at Thanksgiving, birthday, Christmas or Hanukkah
2. birthday gift
3. token of gratitude after special visit
4. group project for sick classmate

How
1. An older member of the family can assemble this kit for a younger family member to make and give as a gift.
2. A child can make a collage picture about himself to give to a close friend or relative.
3. Teens like to glue their memory items onto wine bottles to make bud vases for friendship exchange.
4. For birthday, include snaps of birthday child from birth to now.

Materials
For doing:
  photo of person whose memory story is being created (school photos are perfect)
  frame and mat or poster board with paper frame glued on (8″ × 10″ or larger)
  choice of one or more: old snapshots, magazines, or catalogs to clip, memorabilia (tickets, programs, report cards, matchcovers, etc.)
  glue
  *scissors
For packaging:
  box
  gift wrapping
For directions:
  special occasion greeting card

Assembling
1. Arrange all materials in box and gift wrap.

Directions for Collage Memories in Frames Kit
1. Glue photo on mat, poster board, or other surface provided.
2. Cut out pictures and choose memory items that tell the story of the person in the photo. What are his/her favorite hobbies, foods, sports, entertainments, etc?
3. Piece together, overlapping the pictures and memorabilia and glue your choices around the photo.

Spook Salad-Making Kit

For Halloween or anytime!

Ages 5 and up

Skills

1. nutrition
2. stimulating the sense of taste
3. confidence in the kitchen

When

1. school Halloween party
2. birthday party lunch
3. playgroup or scout cooking project
4. children help at home

How

1. A mother might have this ready for an after-school project and snack for her child's visiting group of friends.
2. Use as a substitute for candy treats at a Halloween party.

Materials:

For making:
favorite fruits and vegetables, such
as:
cucumbers
pineapple
celery
bananas
oranges
carrots
pears
apples
candy corn or miniature marshmallows
raisins
plastic knives
vegetable peeler
*kitchen knives
*cutting board
*large mixing bowl
*spoon
For packaging:
basket or grocery bag
bow
For directions:
1 piece heavy white paper cut into spook shape or other shape to suit the occasion

Assembling

1. Arrange ingredients and any gift utensils in basket or bag.
2. Attach bow and direction sheet to basket handle or outside of grocery bag.

Directions for Spook Salad-Making Kit

1. Peel and dice vegetables with kitchen or plastic knives.
2. Cut fruits into bite-sized pieces.
3. Mix fruit, vegetables, and raisins.
4. Top with sprinkling of candy corn or tiny marshmallows for a festive touch!

Personalized Pencil Case or Book Bag Kit

Adding name or initials is the touch that makes this inexpensive gift special!

Ages 4 and up

Skills
1. labeling
2. eye-hand coordination
3. creating original designs

When
1. birthday or holiday gift
2. bon voyage gift to do in train, plane, or car
3. off-to-school gift
4. take-to-the-hospital activity

How
1. Preschoolers can do this independently using materials where letters are ready to stick and need no cutting.

Materials
For making:
   plastic pencil case or book bag
   choice of one or two for designing bag:
      peel and stick letters
      small roll of colored tape
      contact paper scraps
      peel and stick address labels colored with waterproof markers

optional: pencil case supplies such as:
      ruler
      pencil
      eraser
      crayons
      sharpener
      stencils
      protractor
      scissors

For packaging:
   box or bag
   wrapping (for back-to-school gift wrap, use back-to-school newspaper ads)
   tape

For directions:
   file card or special-occasion greeting card

Assembling
1. If you are using address labels or contact paper, precut for the preschool child or predraw letter shapes for cutting by 6- to 8-year-olds.
2. Wrap the optional pencil case supplies individually for the fun of lots of surprises.
3. Tuck all materials and directions in box or bag. Wrap and tape shut.

Directions for Personalized Pencil Case or Book Bag Kit

1. Make your case special by putting your name or initials on it with peel and stick letters.
2. Add designs around the name on your bag using contact paper or tape.

Candy House Kit

Results SPECTACULAR!

Ages 3 and up

Skills
1. originality
2. accuracy
3. manual dexterity

When
1. holiday remembrance
2. housewarming gift
3. decoration for children's hospital or nursing home
4. benefit raffle or bake sale

How
1. A family can construct the house and join another family to share the trimming! A trip to the candy store to select the goodies is part of the family fun.
2. Older children may cut shapes and gather materials, then help small-fry with assembling, frosting, and decorating.
3. A small group can take pleasure in doing this as a service project.

Materials
For making:
   brown cardboard box, corrugated-type cardboard
   house pattern (p. 108)
   *exacto knife or scissors
   pencil
   ruler
   frosting:
      2 cups confectioners' sugar
      2 egg whites, beaten till a little frothy
      2¼ teaspoons white vinegar or 1 tablespoon lemon juice
1. Put sugar in bowl. Add whites and beat till blended.

2. Add vinegar or lemon juice and beat at high speed 2 minutes till stiff and glossy.

3. Optional: Set aside a small amount and tint green to cover ice-cream cone green for tree by the house.

For giving as a project to complete:
cardboard parts for house (7)
frosting
candy trims such as:
    grape or licorice laces
    spearmint leaves (bushes)
    licorice snaps (good roof)
    cinnamon candies
    silver balls
    Necco wafers (good roof)
    candy corn
    striped gum
    Have fun in the candy store!
house pattern
copy of frosting recipe
plastic knife
shoe box lid
optional: ice-cream cone

For packaging:
frosting container such as margarine tubs, Crisco tin
plastic bags
ribbon
shoe box

For directions:
recipe card decorated with glued-on candy or seasonal card with recipe cards inserted

Assembling

1. Using house pattern, cut house from cardboard with exacto knife or scissors. Label the pieces "floor," "roof" (2), "ends" (2), "sides" (2).

2. Mix frosting and put in airtight container.

3. For children ages 3 to 7, pre-assemble the house, leaving frosting and trimming for child to do (see directions 1–4).

4. Bag trims and place in shoe box with frosting, other materials, and directions. Put lid (with house, if assembled) on shoe box. Tie with bright ribbon.

Directions for Candy House Kit

1. Use butter spreader, plastic knife, and fingers to spread a little frosting on one side of floor piece. Stick down onto top of shoe-box lid.

2. Spread frosting on edges of house walls and ends.

3. Stick side walls, ends, and floor of house together. Use pins to help hold cardboard pieces together. Allow to set.

4. Put frosting on top edges of house and stick roof on.

5. Frost entire house fairly thickly. Frost lid less thickly.

6. Press candy trims onto the house in door and window shapes and fanciful designs. Use green candies for bushes.

7. Cover ice-cream cone with green frosting to make evergreen tree. Press tree onto lid base.

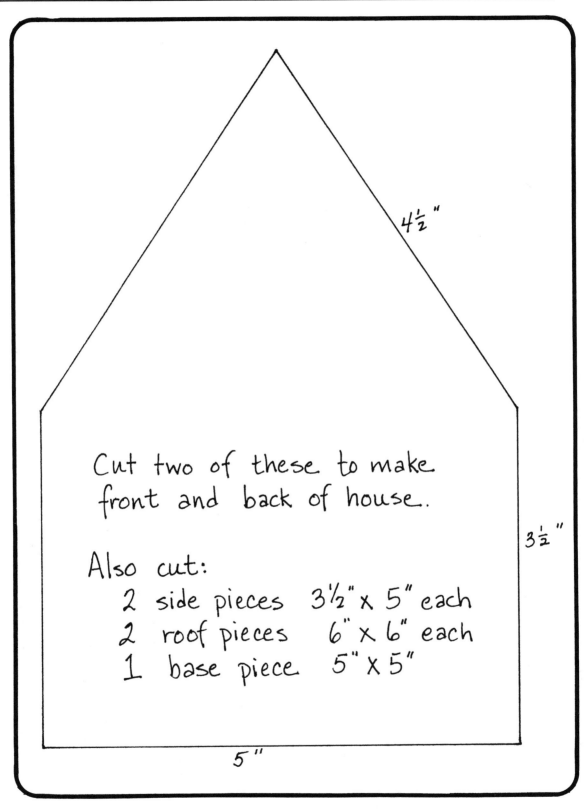

4½ "

Cut two of these to make
front and back of house.

Also cut:
 2 side pieces 3½" x 5" each
 2 roof pieces 6" X 6" each
 1 base piece 5" X 5"

3½ "

5 "

Cookie Cutter Knox Blox Kit

Jiggly treats made in a jiffy!

Ages 3 and up

Skills
1. measuring
2. creativity
3. reading

When
1. special occasion gift
2. entertainment with a young visitor
3. a child's contribution to a potluck supper

How
1. A compact gift which Grandma can assemble and have ready for the grandchildren's visit.
2. Make Knox bloxes in anticipation of playgroup or a preschooler's party. Give each child his own cookie cutter for cutting their own taste treat shapes. Have the recipe ready for all the guests to take home.
3. A sitter can bring the ingredients, make the recipe with the children, then leave a copy of recipe for repeated enjoyment.

Materials
For making:
  3 three-ounce packages flavored Jell-O (color to suit occasion)
  4 envelopes (tablespoons) unflavored gelatin

2 to 3 small cookie cutters (shapes appropriate for time of year)
*4-cup measure
*jelly-roll pan or 9″ × 12″ baking dish
*large spoon
*spatula

For packaging:
  large manila envelope
  markers
  ribbon
For directions:
  recipe card

Assembling
1. Decorate envelope with markers.
2. Place materials with written recipe and directions in envelope.
3. Attach ribbon for gift look.

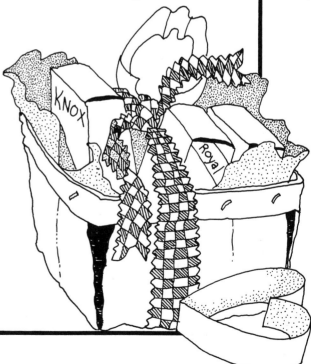

Directions for Cookie Cutter Knox Blox Kit

1. Mix dry Jell-O and unflavored gelatin together in pan.
2. Stir in 4 cups boiling water. Adult help is needed here!
3. Mix completely with spoon until Jell-O has dissolved. Chill a few hours until firm.
4. Use your cutters to cut pretty shapes.
5. Lift out carefully with wide knife or spatula.
6. Nibble the jiggly shapes!
7. Heap leftover gelatin into dishes for a pretty dessert.
8. Another way! *Super Celebration Cake.* Double Knox blox recipe and put into two 9″ cake tins. Chill. Unmold and spread Cool Whip between layers. Decorate top with squirt can whipping cream. Yummmmm!

Family Bouquet Kit

A very personal bouquet.

Ages all ages

Skills
1. combining materials in an original way
2. manual dexterity
3. artistic expression

When
1. for sick teacher or classmate from the "class family"
2. from a family to a bereaved home
3. gift from scout troop, Sunday school, daycare
4. token for nursing home visit
5. welcome for a new baby

How
1. This can be done with a single photo flower tucked in a plant or with a bunch of the flowers arranged in a bouquet.

Materials
For making:
    small individual snapshot of person who will make the flower.
    colored tissue paper
    popsicle stick or coffee stirrer
    potted plant or clay in small basket or container
    oaktag or 3″ × 5″ index card
    glue
    *scissors
    *stapler
For packaging:
    plastic food storage bags
    twist 'ems

box or shopping bag

For directions:

colored paper tag decorated with a flower, cut out or drawn

Assembling

1. Precut and staple for the preschooler (see direction steps 1–4).
2. Put one piece tissue paper, oaktag, one stick, and a photo into each bag and twist 'em. Pack a bag for each participant if you are doing this in a group.
3. Box all materials.

Directions for Family Bouquet Kit

1. Fold tissue paper so there are about 4 layers.

2. Cut an uneven circle shape through the layers (about 4½″ to 5″ diameter). These will be flower petals.
3. Staple through the middle of the pile to hold.
4. Cut circle from oaktag or index card (about 2″ diameter).
5. Glue picture of yourself into oaktag circle, and then glue circle into center of flower.
6. Fluff up edges of each circle of tissue around the photo.
7. "Plant" your flower in the soil of a potted plant (or clay if you are making a bouquet of tissue paper flowers).

Make Your Own Cards Kit

Guaranteed hit! Fun to do! Attractive results!

Ages 3 and up

Skills
1. combining shapes to create designs
2. gluing
3. manipulation

When
1. TV substitute
2. gift for sick child
3. holiday project
4. group activity

How
1. Adult or older child will enjoy making this kit for a preschooler or friend.
2. An ideal activity for grandparents to plan and enjoy doing with their grandchildren.

Materials
For making:
    box of white note cards with envelopes
felt pieces (see "Assembling" and "Directions")
Q-tips or glue brush
white glue
optional: sequins, glitter, ribbon
For packaging:
plastic bag, sandwich size
tape or stapler
optional: gift wrap

For directions:
    white note card decorated with felt shapes and glitter as a sample card

Assembling
1. For preschoolers or the very young: precut felt into shapes; make simple sketches of completed cards for easy copying by child.
2. Put materials into plastic bag and tape or staple shut.
3. Gift wrap if you wish.

Directions for Make Your Own Cards Kit

1. Cut out felt designs. Begin with some of the following ideas:
    stars and moon
    apple and worm
    bubbles with bubble pipe
    sunflower
    mushroom with spots
    ladybug
  Holiday suggestions:
    holly with berries
    chicken with broken egg
    pine tree with balls
    candy cane with bow
    menorah with flames
    hearts in varying sizes

2. Sort out felt cutouts so that pieces for separate cards are in separate piles. Preschoolers should be given one card at a time to do.

3. Glue designs onto note cards. Use an interesting combination of shapes and trims to make your cards original or abstract in design.

4. Give a set of completed cards as a gift. Use some yourself for writing friends.

Clown Kit

Be a clown! All the world loves a clown!

For all ages

Skills
1. interpretation
2. visual communication
3. directional play

When
1. birthday party clown
2. Halloween
3. Scout or school benefit
4. parade
5. surprise from Grandma

How

1. An adult or older child may add spark to a preschool party by appearing in costume to give out balloons or favors, to do magic tricks or just add festive atmosphere to a circus or other party theme.

Materials

For head and face:

hats grown-up's discards, baseball hat, homemade paper cone

wigs cotton batting, mop, inverted paper bag with front cut-out and rest fringed, yarn

frills fake flowers, pom-poms, (p.33), fabric scraps, feathers, paper drawings

makeup makeup discards, burnt cork, paper beak: triangle cut, folded, taped to face, paper moustache, lipstick, eyebrow pencil

mask store-bought, eye mask: glued-on popsicle stick, ping pong ball epoxied on as nose, cut paper

For clothing:

baggy top sweatshirt, pajama

bottoms baggy pants, sweatsuit, pajama

accessories paper drawings, ribbons, pom-poms (p.33), fake flowers, belts, scarves

accordion collar pleated paper made into fan and stapled to a paper strip, or gathered strip of fabric

sewing, gluing, and drawing materials necessary

For packaging:

carton or clothes box

plastic bags

twist 'ems

For directions:

greeting card to suit the occasion or heavy colored paper with clown picture drawn or pasted on

Assembling

1. Label box "Clown Kit."
2. Bag and twist 'em all small parts.
3. Put in box with rest of costume parts.

Directions for Clown Kit

Create your own clown costume!

Robot Costume Kit

Ages 4 and up

Skills
1. initiating imagination
2. artistic expression
3. role playing

When
1. Halloween
2. playgroup
3. costume for dramatic production

How
1. Adult help is necessary for cutting holes and attaching robot's arms.
2. Use to help space enthusiasts transform themselves to another world.
3. A kit that makes it possible for a child to make his own contest-winning costume.

Materials
For making:
  large-size cardboard detergent cylinder (metal base removed) or cardboard box with bottom removed
  dryer hosing (hardware store) equal to double the length of child's arm
  contact paper in various solid colors
  silver spray paint
  white plastic flower pot (rounded at base in size to fit child's head)
  *kitchen knife
  *sharp scissors

For packaging:
  brown grocery bag
  yarn tie (long enough to reach around cylinder)
  *punch
For directions:
  markers for bag decoration

Assembling
1. Cut armholes in cardboard cylinder using kitchen knife. The holes should be slightly smaller than the hosing.
2. Cut two equal lengths of dryer hosing about equal to length of child's arms.
3. Decorate bag with instructions for making robot and illustration of completed costume. Label the bag "ROBOT KIT."
4. Place all items (except cylinder) into the bag. Fold down top of the bag, punch two holes and tie bag to the cylinder.

Directions for Robot Costume Kit

1. Use a variety of contact paper shapes to design front panel on cylinder.

2. Insert dryer hosing into arm holes.

3. Put on costume and invert flower pot and wear on your head to complete robot appearance. Remember to walk like a robot.

Floor Pool Game Kit

Quick to put together and endless fun to play!

Ages 5 and up

Skills
1. measuring
2. eye-hand coordination
3. competition

When
1. welcome-to-our-house activity
2. birthday or holiday token
3. gift to take to a friend and share on the spot
4. to do with a baby-sitter

How
1. Take this kit to share with another family. Children of all ages enjoy playing this together.
2. Assemble this in anticipation of entertaining company, or as a birthday party activity.

Materials
For doing:
  masking tape
  bag of marbles
  tube from roll of gift wrapping or ½″ to ⅜″ dowel, 1 yard long
For packaging:
  wrapping (funny papers are great!)
  tape
For directions:
  greeting card or colored paper

Assembling
1. Roll materials up in wrapping. Tape ends.
2. Tape directions onto package.

Directions for Floor Pool Game Kit
1. Stick a large masking tape circle, measuring 1 yard across, onto carpet or floor.
2. Make a smaller circle, measuring 6″ across, inside the large one. The smaller the circle, the harder the game.
3. Drop marbles into the large circle. Make sure none are in the little circle.
4. *Game Rules.* Easier game for ages 4 to 6: Take turns choosing a marble and "shooting" it toward the small circle with the tube or stick. If the marble lands inside the circle, you keep the marble. Take turns till all the marbles have been won.

   Harder game for ages 7 and up: Take a marble as a "hitting marble." When it is your turn, put the marble someplace on the outline of the large circle in line with a marble you want to shoot into the smaller circle. Use the stick to shoot the "hitting" marble toward the marble you have chosen. If you strike the marble and it goes into the little circle, you "win" the marble. Let everyone have a turn. The winner is the person with the most marbles at the end of the game.

Fireside Kit

A warm way for two families to share a cold day!

For all ages

Skills
1. creative gift giving
2. socialization
3. making selections

When
1. winter house gift for sharing during the visit
2. for an after-skating or sledding party
3. Hanukkah or Christmas gift
4. housewarming gift

How
1. Include in the gift a good balance of things to eat and things to do. Sample Fireside Kit:
   drink mix, cups, cookies, flame color, deck of cards with game rules
2. An older child can work along with a younger one to assemble this family gift.

3. Have each member of the family add his own favorite pastime to the gift.

Materials
For making:

An assortment of home-created treats for a family to share by the fire. Choose from:

To eat:
cocoa (p.67)
M and M Cookies (p.37)
Grandma Stoklosa's Cookie Mix (p.176)
pizza (p.38)
root beer (p.40)
instant s'mores (p.60)

To play:
Clipboard Games (p.191)
Floor Pool Game (p.118)
Party Games (p.120)
Tape Resist Game Board (p.88)
Black and Red Cards (p.168)

To enjoy:
    flame color (p.99)
    long matches
    book or two
    store-bought, long-burning log
    tapes with prerecorded radio
    mystery, sound riddles, original
    ghost stories
        mugs or holiday paper cups to go
        with drink mix
For packaging:
    basket or gift box
    plastic bags and individual boxes
    ribbon
For directions:
    index cards
    greeting card

Assembling

1. Choose taste treats and games to suit the number and ages of people to receive the gift.
2. Separately package the supplies and directions needed for each gift activity.
3. Arrange everything in gift basket or box with cheerful bow and greeting card!

Directions for Card Enclosure for Fireside Kit

a warm message such as:
    "Choose a time to enjoy the fire and family fun!"

Party Game Kit

Quick and easy-to-set-up games for party play.

Ages 4–10

Skills

1. fair play
2. large and small motor skills
3. cooperation

When

1. birthday party
2. playgroup
3. spare-time fun with overnight guests

How

1. For the perfect do-it-yourself birthday, use these games along with the ideas for cake (p.100), ice-cream-cone clowns (p.98), piñata (p.98), and party favor (p.99).
2. Children can add materials for their own game ideas.
3. All ages enjoy gathering game equipment in anticipation of friends coming.

Materials

For playing:
    materials depend on the games cho-

sen, see "directions."

For packaging:

bags or boxes to hold materials for games chosen

gift box to hold everything

wrapping to suit the occasion

For directions:

greeting card

file cards

Assembling

1. Choose materials for an assortment of party games.
2. The materials and directions needed for each idea may be wrapped together or separately. If you wish, include directions and materials for cake, ice-cream-cone clown, piñata, or favor found in Quick Kits section (pp.96–101).
3. Arrange everything in large gift box. Wrap. Label PARTY GAME KIT.

Materials and Directions for Party Game Kit

Sink a Boat

folded newspaper boat (p.158)

permanent marker, pennies

1. Write your name on a boat.
2. Set boat afloat in bathtub with other players' boats.
3. Stand back. Pitch pennies into the other players' boats. Winning boat is the last to stay afloat.
4. Tub cleanup is part of the game!

Circle the Number

newspaper car-sales pages

pencils or markers

1. Agree on a number to look for. Maybe the age of the birthday child! Example: 7.
2. Find and circle the number every place that you can on your page. Time limit 5 minutes! Who has the most?

Memory Guess Tray

assortment of small objects

cloth to cover

tray

1. Arrange objects on tray. Study them.
2. Close your eyes while a leader covers the tray and removes 1 to 2 objects.
3. Open your eyes. Who can say what is missing?

Calendar Toss

page from old calendar

pennies

1. Place calendar page flat on the floor or bed.
2. Take turns trying to hit a number squarely.
3. Add up the numbers you hit to make your "score."
4. Make up new rules and play.

Dice Decide

dice, 1 per child

1. Team up guests in pairs. Throw dice.
2. Use the highest throw to decide order of opening birthday presents or what game to play.

Lighten-Your-Load Help Kit

A child finds joy in giving the gift of time and effort!

Ages 3 and up

Skills
1. motor skills

When
1. special occasion, Mother's or Father's Day
2. birthday gift from child to adult
3. remembrance for elderly neighbor who needs a helping hand

How
1. A grown-up can help a younger child to assemble this kit and set up a "help time" with the person receiving the gift. A very young child should agree to a *brief* help time. Even the most enthusiastic helper will give out after reaching the limits of his attention span.
2. An older child will put together the kit himself and take it to someone who needs help with a job.

Materials
For doing:
Choose materials needed for the job:
   Example:
   paper toweling or newspaper (best!)
   spray window cleaner
   squeegee
optional: special treat to share when the job is done, such as:
cocoa (p.67)
cookies (p.148 and p.176)

For packaging:
   basket, pail or box
For gift enclosure card:
   Notecard enclosure or paper decorated with picture from an ad showing one of the Help Kit products, such as window cleaner.

Assembling
1. Arrange everything prettily in box, pail, or basket.
2. Add pert bow and card enclosure. *Enclosure* for Lighten-Your-Load Help Kit:
Sample: "Here is a promise for an hour of my help on your spring window cleaning. Keep this basket close at hand. We'll plan a time soon to work together!"

Stompers 'n' Stilts Kit

A giant-sized project for giant-sized fun!

Ages: use of stompers, 3 and up; use of stilts, 7 and up; building of stilts, 9 and up

Skills

1. concentration
2. balance
3. left-right coordination

When

1. birthday or holiday gift
2. visit-a-friend gift
3. class gift from teacher

How

1. A child will love taking his gargantuan surprise to a friend to share the making and playing.
2. The stompers are perfect for the preschooler. They are good for leading up to the use of stilts.

Materials

For making stompers:
    2 coffee cans
    string
    masking tape
    nail with large head
    *hammer

For making stilts:
    2 pieces of wood, clean and knot-free, 1½″ × 1½″ × about 1½ times the height of the child receiving the gift. Each piece of wood must have ⅜″ holes drilled through at 6″ intervals for about 30″ from one end. These are for the placement and readjustment of the foot rest.

2 pieces of wood, 1½″ × 3½″ × 6″
Each piece must have a ⅜″ hole drilled completely through the 1½″ × 6″ side. This is for the placement of these pieces as foot-rests on the longer lengths of wood.

Note: Many hardware stores or lumberyards can arrange to do the drilling if you or a neighbor are not equipped. Phone to check.

sandpaper

2 bolts, ⅜″ × 5″ with wood nuts (Ask your helpful hardware man!)

optional: pliers or wrench (with an "on loan" tag if the recipient might not have it)

For packaging:
   plastic bag
   twist 'ems
   string
   large ribbon (old Christmas wreath bow is great!)
   paper bag

For directions:
   file card

Assembling

1. Place sandpaper, nuts, bolts, pliers, and small pieces of wood into plastic bag. Twist 'em shut and tie to large pieces of wood.
2. Put string and cans for stompers into paper bag. Tie bag to the large pieces of wood.
3. Tie huge bow around the pieces of wood.
4. Tie direction card to bow. If this arrangement does not inspire enthusiastic curiosity, what will?

Directions for Stompers 'n' Stilts Kit

Stompers:

1. Turn can upside down. Use the hammer and nail to punch 2 holes —one on each side of can near top.
2. Put string through holes to make a long handle—slightly shorter than your (child's) hand level when you are standing on the can.
3. Do the same to the other can.
4. Put a foot on each can. Hold the string handles tight, one in each hand. Lift the stompers and your feet by pulling up on each loop of string . . . first one foot, then the other.

Stilts:

1. Smooth all corners and edges of wood pieces with sandpaper.
2. Attach wood-block foot piece by using pliers to put bolt through the hole in the stilt and block. Choose a low height off the ground at first.
3. Push wood nut into hole onto bolt. Tighten bolt with pliers.
4. For your first tries, walk on ground —not hard pavement. Might save scraping a knee!

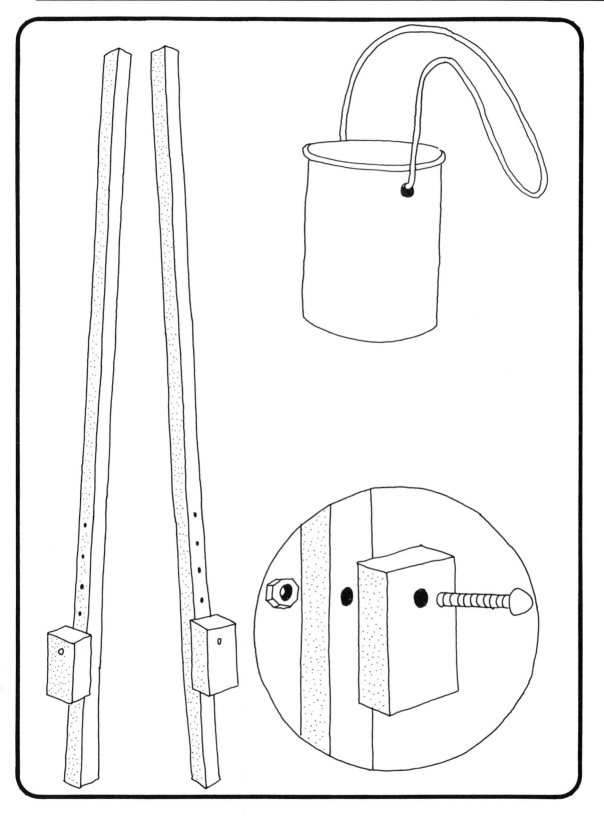

KITS FOR CONFINED SITUATIONS

Chapter 7

Using Kits for Confined Situations

THE MOST TRYING SITUATION of all for adults and children alike is when children must be confined. That circumstance is frequently not a matter of choice—a long anticipated trip is canceled due to sickness; uncooperative weather has meant the postponement of an exciting outing; or a celebration has been canceled abruptly. Original plans have been spoiled and the crestfallen children are at loose ends, if not inconsolable.

Sickness or bad weather compounds the upset of the changed plans, because everyone must stay inside. The result is a disgruntled, trapped feeling. Time suddenly hangs heavy. There can be no new world to conquer by hopping on a bike or into a car to go somewhere. Attitudes begin to be something less than creative.

After the first few minutes of talking out the trouble and upset feelings, what can be done? Quick spontaneous diversions can begin to heal the disappointment and turn attention to pleasanter things. Materials common to the household, quickly gathered, can lead into absorbing play, for example, *Patchwork Scribbles* (p. 134), *Crayon Rubbings* (p. 135), *Playdough Marble Roll Game* (p. 132), or perhaps a kitchen activity.

You would be ahead of the game if a set or two of materials for activities had been tucked away, ready for an unexpected crisis. Working parents are particularly geared to planning at leisure those things that need to be drawn upon in haste.

Maybe you will be lucky enough to avoid unexpected cancellations, but, if you live where there are seasonal changes, you cannot avoid winter which will come with its quota of days spent inside. The period of cold, snow, and short days can be a long harsh one. Winter sports can be enjoyed part of the time, but housebound activities will often be the order of the day.

Activity kits for making a *Bird Feeder* (p. 86) or *Bird Watching* (p. 149) can be set aside for these times. *Shell* (p. 153) or other collections (p. 185) made in summer can be assembled with the necessary materials for cold weather projects. Fingerpainting equipment (p. 66) can be perfect standby fare.

Winter days or unexpected bad weather often force group leaders and teachers to revise plans, too. If you are a playgroup or scout leader, you will have alternate strategies in mind for just such occasions. Plan games to use, projects to do, gifts to make all ready to pull out to fill in the breach.

If you are a teacher, you can always draw on the next assignment in your plan book, but weather problems usually mean a lack of stretched muscles with resulting cobwebby brains and wiggly physiques. Bad-weather options to use for surprises might be *Olympic Games* (p. 90), *Floor Pool* (p. 118), or *Masking Tape Games* (p. 48) which allow for stretching and moving as children divide into groups and set up the activities in different corners of the classroom. Adapt the *Nothing-To-Do Jar* (p. 29) so that it is full of crazy, move-around instructions to be drawn by 2 to 3 children at a time to do—"walk on all fours and bark like a dog," "balance on one foot and sing twinkle twinkle little star," "do jumping jacks while reciting a rhyme." The children will like adding their own silly instructions to the collection in the jar.

In fact, move-around activities should be part of the planning for anyone who needs to deal with the confined child. Children need to stretch their muscles

often and release excess energy.

Sickness presents you with one of the most challenging of all confined situations. Most childhood ailments are thankfully brief, but there may be a period when you are faced with keeping a bedridden child reasonably happy at home or in the hospital. You will be more limited in what you can give a child to do. Quantities of paint spilled over the bedsheets would hardly be appreciated. Your choices will need to be more manageable activities, preferably something that can be worked on, easily set aside, then picked up again later. Such "fill-in" project kits might include *Sewing Cards* (p. 144), *Sparkling Window Shade Pulls* (p. 146), *Pom-Poms* (p. 33), *Cross-Stitch on Gingham* (p. 177), and *Felt-Board Tepee* (p. 156).

There are many opportunities for children, singly or in a group, to create gifts helpful for entertaining a sick friend or sibling. *A Work-and-Play Project Board* (p. 135) is a godsend for moving an ongoing activity out of the way till it can be resumed. It is also the perfect gift for a child to make for his bedridden sister or brother, or hospitalized friend.

A group of children might express their get well wishes with the gift of a decorated clipboard (p. 173) with classmates' autographs signed on the board. Attached to this might be a selection of *Pencil and Paper Games* (p. 191) with additional favorites from members of the group.

To while away long hours *Surprise Kits* (see Going Places, pp. 188) can provide the continuing element of surprise and a good balanced variety of entertainments and learning experiences. Look at the list of ideas and choose an assortment to suit the age and interests of the recipient. Wrap different groupings separately (sample grouping: materials for stencil work—

stencils, crayons, pad of paper). Number each package and let the child open them by number, one a day or one in the morning and one in the afternoon. For the child who enjoys reading, *Book Countdown* (p. 169) can be a variation on this idea. Happy anticipation of any kind makes the day go faster.

During those days when the child is up but not yet playing with friends, kitchen, workshop, or limited outdoor activities become a possibility. Your own backyard may be the boundaries for the convalescent. Being outdoors offers some fresh scenery and an opportunity for some new kinds of kit activities when the usual backyard pastimes have been exhausted. *Pringle's Bug Catcher* (p. 82), homemade bubble-blowing equipment (dishwashing liquid, a little water and toilet tissue tube), or a new pail and one of the household paintbrushes for "painting" the house with water are all possibilities.

During illnesses and convalescence do not overlook those frightening times when a shot must be endured, blood tests taken, or upsetting tests done. These are times when rewards for bravery can brighten spirits, or a new project or game can help make tears disappear.

What if *you* are the one incapacitated? Activity kits drawn from your emergency supply can be a help. If nothing is handy, older children in the family can assemble simple projects for use by the younger fry and for communal play. For your own preservation, encourage the choice of quiet activities or projects that can be picked up, put down, and worked on over a period of time.

If you are up to some entertainment, lend the children tapes and recorder to produce a talent show. At a time when you cannot even cope with meals, draw on

easy cooking ideas (pizza, p. 38), (salad, p. 104) for the family to use while fending for itself.

Sometime you will be on the sidelines watching another family cope with the problems of illness. An activity kit to occupy the children such as *Thumb-and-Fingerprint Doodles* (p. 35) or a remembrance made from one of the project suggestions such as *Family Bouquet* (p. 110) would be welcome gifts.

The arrival of a new baby in a household can mean a time of confinement for family members. It is a divided time for parents caught between baby demands and sibling needs for attention. A simple activity surprise can be used to amuse a sibling at feeding time. Felt boards or puppets allow activity for the child while mother silently participates by listening. The attention-getting device is a constructive one for the older child.

It is also important to consider the older child when the baby is being showered with packages. A simple gift kit can help to make him feel important and offer a diversion with which to busy himself while Mom and Dad are preoccupied with the infant.

Gifts and activity projects given to divert attention from disappointment or confinement need not create an atmosphere of "spoiling" or result in tucking the child off in a corner to entertain himself. A focus on the materials at hand teamed with ideas for using are meant to produce absorbing time fillers. They allow the child to be busy and happy, the parent to continue on with what must be done, and for both to have a feeling of companionship and productive time spent together. A successful effort has been made to soothe the disappointment and/or accept the confinement.

Quick Kits for Confined Situations

Playdough Marble Roll Game

Ages 3 and up

Materials
3–4 marbles
lump of clay or play dough, bought
   or homemade (see recipe, p.96)

Directions
1. Make hill with clay.
2. With your fingers press a path in
the clay along which your marbles
can roll.
3. Make another path. Have marble
races!

Photo Album

Ages 4 and up

Materials
spare photos
album or notebook
rubber cement

Directions
Arrange and glue photos in the
   album to tell a story about yourself.

Map Fun

Ages 7 and up

Materials
world or United States map
envelopes with distant postmarks or
   return addresses
tape or straight pins
*scissors

Directions
1. Hang the map if you wish.
2. Cut out postmarks and return addresses. On the map find the places
where they came from. Pin or tape
them to those spots.

Light-Up Electric Fun

Ages 7 and up

Materials

2 or more flashlight batteries, the same or different sizes

insulated wire with short length of wire exposed at ends

flashlight bulb

clear and masking tapes

Directions

1. Tape two batteries together so that the negative (smoothest) end of one is touching the positive end of the other.
2. Use clear tape to attach bulb to the positive end of these two batteries.
3. Tape one end of a piece of wire to the negative end of the line of batteries. Touch the other end of the wire to the metal side of the light bulb. The bulb will light.
4. Add more batteries. Tape the wire to the end of the longer line and light the bulb. Is it brighter? Try different combinations of batteries.

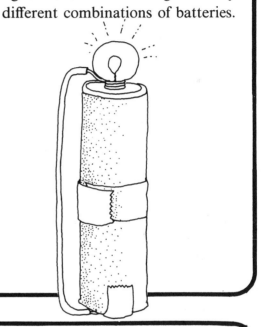

Color Play

Ages 3 and up

Materials

pairs of sample paint chips in an assortment of colors (from hardware store or decorator)

Directions

1. If you are age 3 to 6, arrange the color chips so they are in matched pairs.
2. If you are age 7 or up, arrange the color chips "rainbow" fashion. Colors will go from yellow to green to blue to purple to red to orange and back to yellow.
3. Extra! Get together paper and glue for a color chip design-making project.

Patchwork Scribbles

Ages 4 and up

Materials
pad of unlined paper
colorful markers

Directions
1. With one marker make a large-spaced scribble pattern.
2. Fill each space with a special design. Use dots, circles, Xs, zigzags, etc.

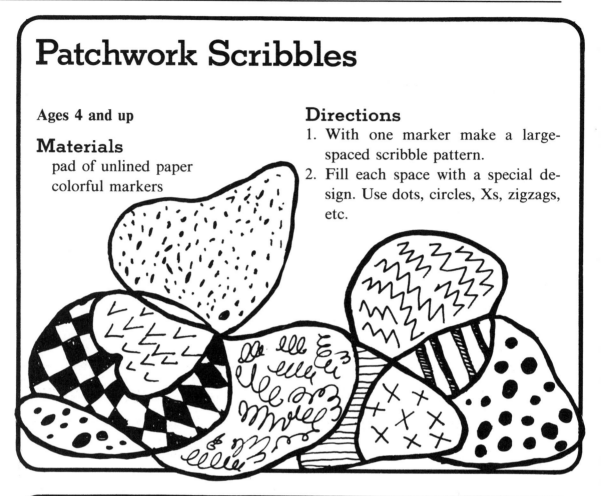

Magnifying Magic

Ages 3 and up

Materials
magnifying glass
textured objects such as:
    orange slice
    sandpaper
    soil
    fur
    eraser
    toothbrush

Directions
1. Examine textured objects through the magnifying glass.
2. Add other objects to your collection for inspection.

Crayon Rubbings

Ages 4 and up

Materials

crayons with paper wrapping removed

newsprint or drawing paper

flat objects plucked from drawers or nature, such as:

    rubber magnet

    leaf

    row of unused twist 'ems

    coins

    paper clips

Directions

1. Sandwich objects between two pieces of paper. Clip together.
2. Rub over the entire object with the side of a crayon.
3. Watch the imprint appear on your paper.
4. Use your rubbing patterns for notepaper or gift wrap.

Work-and-Play Project Board

Ages 7 and up

Materials

scrap of paneling or other thin board, about 18″ × 36″

masking tape, strong and wide

leftover paint—spray paint or can with brush

Directions

1. Paint the unfinished sides of the board.
2. Put tape around edges for finishing. You have a neat project board!
3. Use for art, Lego building, stamp sorting and other projects in bed, on the floor, in front of the TV. It is easy to pick up your project board to set aside for a later play session.

Spotlight Game

Ages 3 and up

Materials
flashlight
poster with lots of interesting things pictured on it, e.g., Disney World map

Directions
1. Hang poster and darken room.
2. Use the flashlight to spotlight all the things that are alike. For example: all the plants, all the animals, or all the buildings.

Recording

Ages 4 and up

Materials
tape recorder (on loan)
choose one or more:
  blank tape
  story cassettes with book (library, store)
  other cassettes: music, travel guides, humor
  Guessing Sounds Cassette (p.137)

Directions
1. Rehearse songs; make up plays; read stories; invent sound games; play an instrument. Record some of these on tape.
2. Listen to ready-made and home-made tapes.

Squiggle Story Notebook

Ages 6 and up

Materials
notebook with squiggle lines drawn on several left-hand pages and labeled "Squiggle Story Notebook"
crayons

Directions
1. Look at a squiggle line.
2. Make a picture using the line as part of your drawing.
3. Write a line or two about your drawing on the opposite page.
4. Make new squiggle lines and drawings.

Activity Kits for Confined Situations

Guess the Sounds and Tunes Kit

Fun with a tape recorder!

Ages 4 and up

Skills
1. auditory discrimination
2. listening
3. sound communication

When
1. traveling
2. sick at home
3. small group activity

How
1. An adult and child or two older children can prepare a tape in anticipation of enjoying a guessing game with a friend.
2. A large group of children will enjoy dividing into two teams—one tapes mystery sounds and the other tries to guess.
3. A family will enjoy preparing a guessing tape to be mailed as a gift to a distant friend.

Materials
For making tape:
    cassette tape
    records, familiar songs, and nursery
      rhymes without the words
    tape recorder (loan)
    *record player
For packaging:
    basket or box
    bow

For directions:
    cassette tape or construction paper

Assembling
1. Record directions on tape.
2. Record a variety of different sounds such as: ticking clock, beater, baby rattle, jingling keys, dial toy or telephone, running water. Record some well-known tunes without words.
3. Announce a number for each sound or piece of music to make identification easier. Leave some space on the tape. A child receiving this gift will want to experiment with recording sounds.
4. Write an identification answer sheet.
5. Place recorder, tape, and answer sheet into basket or box. Add bow.

Directions for Guess the Sounds and Tunes Kit
1. Listen to each sound and guess what it is. Check your answers with the answer sheet.
2. Record new sounds of your own on the tape.
3. For variety, go outside and record sounds you hear around your yard or in the city streets.
4. Play the sound guessing game with a friend.
5. Start a tape exchange with a friend.

Cloth Flowers

Bouquets for every season!

Ages 8 to adult

Skills

1. manipulation
2. color perception and coordination
3. originality

When

1. continuing activity during inside days
2. special occasions—party favors, package decorations
3. recovering from sickness

How

1. Younger children need a helping hand preparing and doing cloth flowers.
2. An older child can assemble this as a project-doing gift for a friend.

Materials

For making:
    colorful fabric scraps
    cotton-covered wire, purchased at hobby shop or dimestore
    flower centers (pistils and stamens), purchased at hobby shop
    florist's clay
    roll of florist's tape
    spool of medium-weight florist's wire
    white glue
    container
    *wire clippers
    *small pointed sharp scissors
For packaging:
    2 plastic bags
    twist 'ems
    gift box
    wrapping
    sample cloth flower
For directions:
    greeting card to suit the occasion

Assembling

1. Cut wire into 4″ lengths (for medium-size petal). Twist each wire length into petal shape. Each petal will look like a loop with a tail. The "tail" is where you have twisted the ends of the wire together. Make four petals for one flower.
2. Cut 4 fabric scraps each slightly larger than a single wire petal.
3. Package petal-shaped wires, centers, and fabric scraps in plastic bag and twist 'em closed.
4. Cut florist wire in 2½″ lengths for stems. Bag with florist tape.
5. Put bags and remaining materials into gift box. Wrap and use a sample flower in place of bow!

Directions for Cloth Flower Kit

1. Glue around the edge of each petal-shaped wire. Press wire onto a piece of fabric. Four matching petals make one flower.
2. Repeat this to make the number of flowers needed for favors or bouquet.
3. Glued petals must dry overnight.

4. Cut around each petal right next to the wire to trim off excess fabric.
5. Join 4 petal "tails" and flower center. Attach florist wire for stem. Twist florist tape around the wire to cover it completely.
6. Open out the petals of each flower.
7. To make a bouquet: Place clay in the bottom of your container. Have fun arranging!

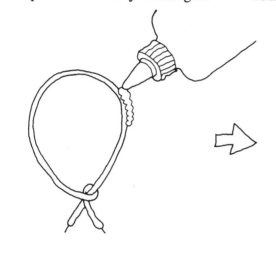

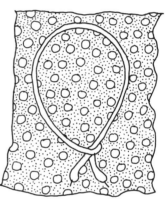

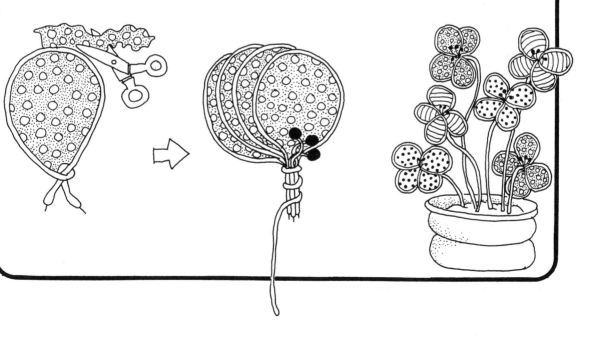

Miniature Scene Kit

Children love to receive miniatures. Add props and turn the gift into a creative project!

Ages 4 and up

Skills

1. creative design
2. space relationships
3. imaginative interpretation

When

1. sick at home
2. house gift needed to share with host
3. classroom spare time

How

1. Older children will love to gather parts for this gift kit to present a younger family member or friend.
2. A teacher can keep a supply of props and boxes on hand for spare-time creativity.

Materials

For making forest scene:
  miniature koala or other bear, preferably with arms that spring together, clip fashion; or other wild animal
  box with lid (doubles for packaging)
  glue
  forest background drawn or cut from wallpaper book or magazine
  small branch to fit box width
  assortment of natural materials; sand, stones, twigs, dried flowers, weeds, etc.
  lump of clay, ¾ size of golf ball
  twist 'ems
Other scene ideas:
  miniature mouse with small box to make table, fabric for tablecloth, bottle caps for dishes, wallpaper, etc.
  Star Wars characters or Super Heroes with appropriate magazine picture or wallpaper for background, different colors of clay for terrain, etc.
  Other miniatures, cars, china animals, figurines, etc., can all be gifts that provide a central figure for a scene project.
For packaging:
  contact paper or wrapping with theme to suit the scene, such as jungle
  ribbon
For directions:
  card with jungle or forest theme

Assembling

1. Cut scene to fit bottom of box.
2. Wrap miniature.
3. Cover outside of box with contact paper or wrapping.
4. Put all materials into scene box with direction card. Be sure to adjust directions to chosen materials. Top with lid and tie.

Directions for Miniature Scene Kit

1. Make a home for your bear! Glue background to inside bottom of box.
2. Stand box on end so background is upright.
3. Press lump of clay in bottom or put holes in top and bottom of scene to insert branch.
4. Clip or twist 'em koala or other animal to branch.
5. Stand branch in clay or insert into hole punched into box "ceiling."
6. Arrange natural materials to complete scene.

Plant a Desert Kit

Maybe the cactus will burst into bloom or have "babies!"

Ages 4 and up

Skills
1. artistic experimentation
2. manual dexterity
3. planning a pattern

When
1. adult, housebound or in nursing home
2. small group
3. rainy day
4. birthday gift

How
1. If you are doing this with pre-schoolers, two children are plenty. Older children, like those in a scout group, can be managed with words of caution about joggling the sand designs.
2. An Arizona traveler might plan on sharing the trip by giving this gift with cactus purchased while traveling or on arrival home.
3. An older child can make two kits to enjoy doing with a special friend.

Materials
For making:
   small cactus
   small jar, about 2-cup capacity—a peanut butter jar or an apothe-

cary jar for a fancy touch
sand in 2 to 3 colors, about ⅓ cup of each, available at hobby shops
optional: For textured instead of colored effect use plain sand, pebbles, or crushed stone (bright white is nice) available from garden shops, your sandbox, the driveway (maybe a friendly neighbor will sacrifice a few handfuls of material . . . ASK FIRST!)
1 cup potting soil
plastic fork
   plastic spoon
For packaging:
   2 to 3 small plastic bags
   twist 'ems
   small basket or box
For directions:
   notecard or postcard decorated with cutout or drawn desert scene

Assembling
1. Put sand in plastic bags and twist 'em shut.
2. Arrange cactus in basket or box with other items placed prettily around it.
3. Tuck in instruction card.

Directions for Plant a Desert Kit

READ DIRECTIONS CARE-FULLY.

1. You might want to run a test before you use the kit materials. Get a tiny, clear container such as a baby jar and 2 to 3 of the following: sugar, instant tea, pepper, salt. Make layers in the jar as in steps 2–4.

2. Now, ready for project doing! Spoon a layer of sand into the jar.

3. If you are 7 or older, use the pencil to make several dents in the sand right next to the glass.

4. Spoon another layer of different colored sand into the jar. If you made dents, you will see an interesting design.

5. Make more layers, each with dent patterns along the edge, till the sand is used up. Make sure there is still enough room to plant the cactus.

6. Add soil.

7. Remove the cactus from its container. A fork will do the job so you will not get prickled. Plant it in the soil.

8. Water lightly. Water again only now and then. Cacti are used to long periods without water.

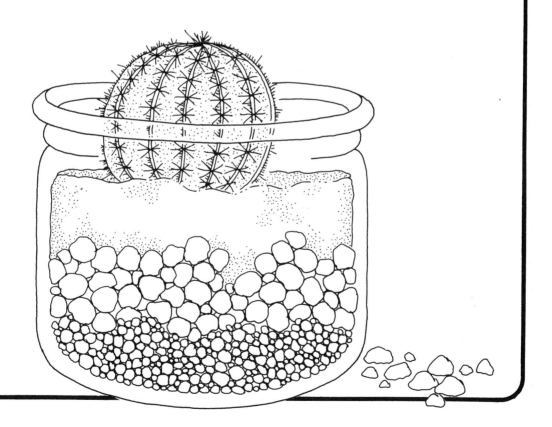

Sewing Card Kit

Ages 3 and up

Skills

1. perceptual coordination
2. strengthening fine motor control
3. recycling

When

1. while waiting—appointments, carpooling, traveling
2. while watching TV
3. get-well gift
4. group project

How

1. A young child will find stitching a frame or outline enough of a challenge. Older children might fill in objects and details using several colors and different weights of yarn.

Materials

For making:

greeting cards: Children's cards of stiff paper in perky shapes (Easter bunnies, birthday bears, chubby snowmen) are best. Good are: shapes cut from adult cards, such as a Christmas tree. Whole rectangular cards are fine for punching and sewing a "frame" around the edge.

several strands of yarn

needlepoint needle

hole punch (available in different sizes)

For packaging:

box

wrapping

yarn

For directions:

greeting card to suit the occasion (can be part cut from an old one)

Assembling

1. For preschoolers prepunch cards and tie yarn. See directions, steps 1 and 2.
2. Put all materials in the box with the instruction card. Wrap prettily, tying with yarn that can be saved for card sewing.

Directions for Sewing Card Kit

1. Use punch to make holes to outline a figure on a card or to punch a frame around the edge of larger cards.
2. Tie yarn through two holes. Make a knot on the back.
3. Stitch from hole to hole all the way around the outline or frame.
4. When you have gone all the way around the outline you can tie the yarn to finish or sew back in the opposite direction to fill in all the spaces.
5. For an extra challenge punch details. Fill in with a variety of colors.
6. Share these gift pictures with special people you know—as a greeting card for a friend or a present to Grandad.

Sparkling Window Shade Pull Kit

Foolproof and the results are so pretty!

Ages 3 and up

Skills

1. shape recognition
2. planning a pattern
3. grouping objects

When

1. sick in bed
2. Mother's Day or teacher gift
3. family project for holiday gift giving
4. scout or brownie project

How

1. Abstract or realistic shapes of all sorts can be made. At Christmas, make candy canes or wreaths for the tree. Pretty to hang in the window or please the eye.
2. Have scouts or playgroup do and give to someone in a nursing home. Deliver personally to add meaning.

Materials

For making:

28 cartwheel beads (from hobby shop); choose colors to suit the room where pull will go.

8 facet beads; you may choose some other bead combination—enough to cover about 7″ on a pipe cleaner.

1 pipe cleaner

1 20″ piece of string, yarn, or fish line

For packaging:

small box

ribbon

For directions:

paper cut to size of box lid

felt pen

Assembling

1. Write directions on paper and glue inside or on top of lid.
2. Put all materials in box.
3. Tie with festive ribbon.

Directions for Sparkling Window Shade Pull Kit

1. Bend one end of the pipe cleaner so that the beads will not slip off.
2. String the beads in a pretty pattern —4 cartwheels, then 1 facet, until all the beads are used.
3. Bend the finished piece into a circle and twist the pipe cleaner ends together in a bow shape.
4. Tie string in a long loop through the pull, ready for hooking to a window shade.

Paper Doll Set Design Kit

Both boys and girls love to do this!

Ages 5 and up

Skills
1. cutting
2. creative thinking
3. directional play

When
1. surprise for restless times
2. get-well gift
3. small group or classroom activity

How
1. Use an old wallpaper book to create settings for paper doll play.
2. Children enjoy creating scenes and easily become involved in flights of fancy and dramatic play.

Materials
For doing:
  discarded wallpaper book (from hardware store or decorator) or large sheets cut from leftover rolls
  catalogs (Sears, Ward's, department store, gift mail order)
  furniture advertising fliers
  fabric scraps
  scissors
  paste
  pencils, crayons, or markers
  optional: paper doll book

For packaging:
  large shopping bag
  tape
  rubber bands
For directions:
  colored paper or file card

Assembling
1. Roll and secure wallpaper pages with rubber band.
2. Put all materials in shopping bag.
3. Label bag "Design Kit."
4. Tape directions to bag.

Directions for Paper Doll Set Design Kit
1. Use wallpaper pages as backgrounds for different scenes.
2. Cut and paste or draw features like windows and doors to create settings for house, office, store, beach, disco club, etc.
3. Cut out furniture and accessories (lamps, curtains, etc.) and add to your set design.
4. Use sets as backdrops for paper doll play and stories. Play flat or tape backdrop to wall.
5. Change paper doll clothes to suit the background.

Paintbrush Cookies Kit

"Kitchen Artists" will want this to become a holiday tradition.

Ages 3 and up

Skills
1. following directions
2. painting
3. interpretation

When
1. reward (for a great report card, bravery at the doctor's office)
2. playgroup
3. school party
4. tea with a "shut-in" neighbor
5. gift tags or ornaments

How
1. Package as a kit for doing when the family visits grandparents or friends for the weekend.
2. A preschooler will like helping Mom make the cookie dough and then take as a kit gift for a friend who is housebound.
3. Cookies are made and kit assembled in anticipation of "your day" to have playgroup.

Materials
For painting:
  sugar cookie dough (made from any basic recipe or premixed dough from grocer's dairy section)
  special cookie cutters
  egg yolk paint

Completely blend 2 egg yolks and ½ teaspoon of water.
  Divide into 4 jars. Add drops of food coloring to each jar till color is bright.
  small, new paintbrushes (at least one per child)
  water dish
  paper towels
  baby food jars, one for each color of egg yolk paint
  *rolling pin
  *spatula
For packaging:
  airtight container for cookie dough
  small box for paint supplies
  ribbon
For directions:
  felt pen
  paper cut to size of box lid

Assembling
1. Package cookie dough in separate container.
2. Mix egg yolk paint in individual jars.
3. Place paint jars, brushes, paper towels, and water dish in box.
4. Write paint recipe and directions on paper and glue on box top.
5. Tie ribbon and attach personalized gift tag.

Directions for Paintbrush Cookies Kit

1. Roll out cookie dough to ¼″ and cut shapes. Place on a cookie sheet.
2. Fill your water dish and have paper towels ready. Your brush must be cleaned each time you change color or your results will not be bright.
3. Use your imagination to paint designs and details on the cookies.
4. If paint thickens, add a few drops of water.
5. Refrigerate any leftover paint.
6. Bake cookies according to recipe directions.
7. Use as a decoration or enjoy eating!

Bird Watching Kit

An interest that all ages can enjoy separately and share together!

Ages 3 and up

Skills

1. observation
2. identification
3. learning to record experience

When

1. sick at home
2. reward
3. group or family outing—picnic, hike, campout
4. special occasion gift
5. going-away gift for those headed on a nature-centered vacation

How

1. Young children think of birds as friends and take interest in watching them feed. *Pretend Binoculars* (p. 171) will add to the fun and make them feel *sooo* important!
2. Older children may enjoy the loan of opera glasses or binoculars to help measure their interest in bird watching before making a major investment.

Materials

For making:
  paperback bird identification book; Golden series is inexpensive and good
  marker
  binoculars or opera glasses on loan and/or materials for child's pretend binoculars. (See p. 171)

For packaging:
  gift box
  wrapping with bird theme
  ribbon

For directions:
  notepaper with bird theme

Assembling

1. Wrap individual materials—great for group unveiling!
2. Arrange all materials and directions, including those for pretend binoculars, in gift box. Wrap and tie.

Directions: for Bird Watching Kit

1. Watch for birds from your window, on neighborhood walks, on hikes in the woods. Peer through binoculars, real or pretend, and stalk birds!
2. Match the bird you see to its picture in the book. Put an X beside the picture.
3. Count your Xs from time to time to see how many birds you have spotted!
4. Learn the name of the bird if it is new to you.

Flashlight Planetarium Kit

You are in charge of the stars that light your way!

Ages 8 and up

Skills
1. reference skills
2. following directions
3. observation and identification

When
1. hospitalized child
2. travel gift for camping trip
3. house gift for overnight invitation
4. scout project

How
1. Younger children will enjoy making light patterns through punched holes without any connection to star formations.
2. Older children might develop a code system for late night conversation on a bedroom wall or tent top.

Materials
For making:
  1-pound can
  supply of plastic covers to fit
  hole punch (star-shaped ones are available)
  black acrylic paint
  paintbrush
  chalk
  flashlight
  astronomy book (Choose one that is appropriate to the activity and child's age—*Stars,* by Zim and Baker, published by Golden Press, is good)
For packaging:
  box
  wrapping—shelf or other plain paper with gummed star decorations
For directions:
  index card or blue paper with hand-drawn or gummed stars

Assembling
Place all items in box and wrap.

Directions for Flashlight Planetarium Kit
1. Remove second end from empty 1-pound can.
2. Paint plastic covers black.
3. Use chalk to mark spots on the *inside* of each cover to match different star formations, such as the Big Dipper. Use your star book to help.
4. Punch holes where each mark is.
5. Put lid on a can end. Put lighted flashlight into open end. Shine light through blackened lid with punched holes and watch your constellation appear on bedroom wall or tent top.
6. Learn the names of some constellations.

Hang-Your-Jewels Holder Kit

A portable workshop!

Ages 4 and up

Skills
1. measuring
2. decorating
3. eye-hand coordination

When
1. scout project
2. birthday gift
3. gift to make for Mother's day

How
1. One child can make the holder to give another child. Include in the package recycled costume jewelry or the materials for making a macaroni or bead necklace.
2. Preschoolers will need supervision. Older children will do the project independently.

Materials
For making:
3″ × 12″ wood strip
stain, paint, or spray paint—leftovers are fine
2 screw-type plaque hangers (from hardware or hobby shop)
5 to 6 cup hooks
sandpaper
Deft or clear spray
nail
pencil
paintbrush (loan)
decorations, choice of: peel and stick letters   magic markers   shrink art designs   paint
*hammer

For packaging:
lidded jars in which to put small quantities of paint or stain
cardboard box

For directions:
file card or back of new piece of sandpaper

Assembling
1. Do step 6–7 of directions for preschooler.
2. Place all materials and directions in box. Tag any items on loan with "please return" label.
3. In large letters, label the box "PORTABLE WORKSHOP."

Directions for Hang-Your-Jewels Holder Kit:
1. Sand wood strip.
2. Brush on stain or paint, or spray paint. Dry.
3. Decorate your plaque with name and designs.
4. Put on clear finish with spray or brush.
5. Hammer plaque hanger onto back side.
6. Draw a dot on each spot where you are going to place a cup hook hanger. You will have 5 to 6 dots spaced evenly apart across the center of the board.

7. Hammer a nail separately into each dot, just enough to make a tiny hole.
8. Screw cup hooks into holes.

Shell Identification Kit

A warm way to share a seaside visit with a friend.

Ages 3 and up

Skills

1. scientific observation
2. categorization
3. drawing conclusions
4. recognition of likenesses and differences

When

1. family sharing on a rainy day at the seaside
2. sickness—adult or child
3. scout or playgroup project
4. classroom

How

1. Even a very small child who cannot read is spellbound holding and feeling a shell while exploring the pages of a shell book for the perfect match!
2. Giving this gift kit is one way for grandparents to share their trip to an exotic place with their grandchildren or for a grandchild to share his seashore visit with a grandparent confined to a nursing home.
3. For teachers this kit can be in the corner of the classroom. In spare moments children can add to a classroom master chart of shells—identifying, gluing, labeling.

Materials

For doing:

paperback shell identification book

bag of shells collected on your seaside treasure hunt or from an interesting shop visited on your trip

poster board, about 11″ × 18″—size depends on number of shells

pencil or marker

white glue

For packaging:

onion bag or plastic bag

wrapping with beach theme, such as drawings of boats, shells, or fish on plain paper

yarn or ribbon

For directions: piece of poster board cut in shape of scallop shell or fish

Assembling

1. Wrap book and marker.
2. Put book, marker, and shells in bag and tie shut.
3. Roll up poster board and tie.
4. Tie bag to ribbon on poster board and attach directions.

Directions for Shell Identification Kit

1. Pick a shell from the bag and match it to a picture in the shell book.
2. Glue the shell to the poster board.
3. Print the name of the shell beneath it. If you cannot read or write yet, let an older member of your family write and say the name of the shell. Then you will remember what it is when you see it again!
4. Do the same thing with other shells.

Wood Pieces Kit

Woodworking without a hammer!

Ages 3 and up

Skills

1. clever use of scrap materials
2. size and shape relationships
3. combining groups of objects

When

1. I-don't-know-what-to-do times
2. small group project
3. special occasion gift

How

1. A child has fun gathering the parts of this kit to give to or share with a friend.
2. Use this in a group where there is a wide range of abilities. Some children will make recognizable pictures, others abstract designs. The results are always effective.

Materials

For making:

stiff cardboard, plywood, or particle board, 10″ × 14″ is good

smaller wood scraps (bags of scraps are available where lumber is sold)

white glue

glue brush

jar lid or margarine tub

paint or stain (colored stains are available, several colors are fun)

paintbrush

hanger; plaque hanger or wire/ string, screw eyes, and hook

optional: oddments such as buttons, bottle caps, screws, anything with interesting shape or texture to further decorate wood creation

optional: clear spray or Deft

For packaging:

box

onion bag or plastic drawstring bag

plastic bags

twist 'ems

ribbon or fabric strip with pinked edges for large bow

For directions:

file card

Assembling

1. Put wood pieces in onion or other bag.
2. Put decorative oddments, brushes, and hanging equipment into plastic bags and twist shut.
3. Arrange bags with directions in box. Tie with gift bow.

Directions for Wood Pieces Kit

1. Paint or stain the wood pieces. (This is nice way to extend activity for older children.)
2. Squeeze some glue into lid or container.
3. Brush glue onto wood pieces and press onto the wood or cardboard background to make a design. Glue on buttons or other odds and ends for added detail. Your design can just be interesting shapes or a picture of something special like a boat or robot.
4. Optional: Brush or spray on clear finish. Dry
5. Attach hanger.

Felt-Board Tepee Kit

Fun for two. A wonderful learning exchange!

Ages 4 and up

Skills
1. visual communication
2. sequence
3. word and number associations

When
1. project for two friends housebound by weather
2. for child with new baby at home
3. car travel
4. classroom/daycare spare time

How
1. Preschooler can make stories using just basic geometric felt shapes.
2. Preschoolers will need help cutting extra felt shapes.
3. Older children enjoy felt pieces cut to represent characters in a familiar story.

Materials
For making:
    4 joined sides of a square cardboard box
    large piece of felt to cover two cardboard sides
    felt scraps
    index cards, paper dolls, and/or old greeting cards
      felt pen

    white glue
    *stapler or masking tape
    *scissors (sharp shears needed to cut cardboard and felt)
    optional: sandpaper
For packaging:
    plastic bags
    twist 'ems
    yarn tie or pinked fabric strip
For directions:
    construction paper backed with felt

Assembling
1. Cut one fold on cardboard box so that sides lay flat.

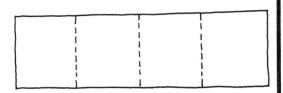

2. Lift up center fold and turn under and overlap the 2 ends so they form a tepee shape.

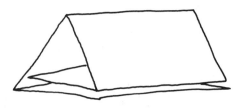

3. Staple or tape together the double thickness on the bottom.
4. Cut large piece of felt to fit outside of 2 slanting sides. Glue on.
5. Cut felt remnants into geometric shapes and/or figures. Include extra felt scraps so that more pieces can be cut by tepee owner. Place all felt in plastic bag and twist closed.
6. Cut and glue strips of felt or sandpaper to index cards, paper dolls, or old greeting cards. Bag in plastic and twist shut.
7. Tie yarn or fabric "ribbon" around center pointed fold to make bow.
8. Attach plastic bags to bow. Place felt-backed direction card on the board.

Directions for Felt-Board Tepee Kit

Enjoy your felt board in lots of ways:
1. Use felt squares, circles, and other geometric shapes to make objects such as houses, people, cars. Tell about them.
2. Make a design with the shapes. See if you or a friend can make a matching design on the other side of the tepee. The more shapes you use the harder it will be for you or a friend to match on the other side.
3. Use paper dolls or greeting cards to tell a story. If you are age 8 or older, on index cards write the story or words the paper dolls speak.
4. For children 6 and up: Try a little math. Place 7 circles on the board. Take away 4. What is left? Write the number story $7 - 4 = 3$. Try other number stories. Invent some math games.
5. Add to your scrap collection and think up new ways to use your Felt Board Tepee.

Newspaper Boat-Folding Kit

You'll be amazed at how long these simple boats stay afloat!

Ages 6 and up

Skills
1. following directions
2. manual dexterity
3. precision and accuracy

When
1. child with new baby at home
2. get-well entertainment
3. visit-a-friend gift
4. birthday party

How
1. Read the story *Curious George Rides a Bike,* by H.A. Rey, published by Houghton Mifflin, to stir interest in boat folding.
2. Make one boat and give with a newspaper supply to a friend planning a party. Folding a fleet of boats for favors will ease that hard-to-wait time before the celebration.
3. Plan paper boat-making when a pal comes to play. Showing a friend "how" is part of the pleasure and accomplishment of this activity.

Materials
For making:
    one double newspaper sheet per boat
    waterproof magic marker
    optional: supply of pennies for game

    optional: book— *Curious George Rides a Bike,* by H.A. Rey, published by Houghton Mifflin Co.
For packaging:
    box
    newspaper for wrapping
    ribbon
    folded boat for gift tag
    optional: margarine tub with lid, for pennies
For directions:
    heavy paper glued to single sheet of newspaper
    optional: newspapers folded to show each step of boat making; important only if you are mailing the kit and cannot be on hand to show the steps in folding

Assembling
1. Place inside the box: boats folded at various stages in making, marker, pennies, directions for making, and *Sink a Boat* game (p.121).
2. Wrap box. Attach sample boat with child's name marked on it.

Directions for Newspaper Boat-Folding Kit

1. IMPORTANT to your success: Be *sure* to match corners evenly; crease each new fold carefully.

2. Fold a full double sheet of newspaper in half.

3. With center fold at the top, fold top corners toward the center until they meet and are equal in size.

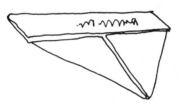

4. Fold bottom edge up on each side. Stop here for hat.

5. Open hat shape and bring ends together. Tuck in loose paper and flatten sideways. Shape is now a diamond.

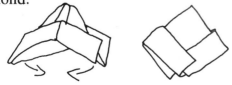

6. Turn bottom point up on each side. Shape is now triangle.

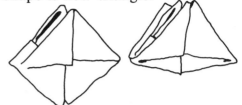

7. Again open hat shape. Bring ends together and flatten.

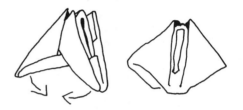

8. Gently pull down end points. Roll in center sides. Your boat is ready for water—sink, bathtub, puddle, river, ocean! Play *Sink a Boat* (p.121).

9. If you are at the beach, have a race with friends. If a boat goes to sea, make another!

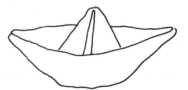

KITS FOR
GOING PLACES

Chapter Eight

Using Kits for Going Places

GOING PLACES WITH CHILDREN is a daily occurrence. There are appointments, carpooling commitments, visits to friends, short excursions with family or groups, and major vacation trips. We are continually on the move with our youngsters, and the list of destinations and various engagements is endless.

Whatever the reason for being on the go, you find yourself continually challenged with making the experience happy or at least tolerable for the children sharing the time with you. The younger the children, the more demanding the undertaking.

Certainly the long car trip requires the most forethought. A little preplanning for the children can make the difference between an adventure to remember and a nightmare of jangled nerves.

Children will want to help plan their own entertainment—gathering up, in no time, all the toys in sight. You will be forced to chop the pile to more portable size amid protests regarding the elimina-

tion of several dozen "favorites." To avoid the problem, begin by agreeing on a bag for each child—a sturdy overnight case, tote, backpack, or other small bag. Let each child know that this is his travel kit and that his own share of toy choices is limited to the size of the particular bag assigned.

A preschooler will need some help. Make sure a favorite stuffed toy is included, and choose two or three of the toys that will give the best playing value in the cramped surroundings of the car. Avoid things with lots of loose pieces and anything that is a noisemaker.

Older children might need a word or two of advice. Suggest a good balance such as a book, some handiwork, pencil and paper work, a favorite game, items to enjoy at your destination, and something the youngster remembers enjoying on the road during the last trip.

Use the time of anticipation to advantage. Children will like taking part in the cooking end of travel plans. Taste treats such as *M and M Cookies* (p. 37) and *Grandma Stoklosa's Cookies* (p. 176) can be made in advance and enjoyed en route.

Another pretrip project is making thank-you gifts for people you are visiting during your travels. Ideas for the youngest *Instant Wall Hanging* (p. 65), to the oldest *Linoleum Block Prints* (p. 27), combine the talents and enthusiasm of everyone to fill a "hard-to-wait" period of time.

Older children can even make a game or two to take along, for example, *Battleship* (p. 182) for themselves or *Color Testers* (p. 172) to share with younger members of the family.

The trip will offer an opportunity for the different ages to play together since the close quarters make it impossible to ignore one another or go off in opposite directions as they might normally do. Elder brothers and sisters may find themselves enthusiastically playing games they might consider quite babyish any other time.

The most successful of all travel aids is the *Going-Places Surprise Kit* (p. 188). It has been a standby for many a journeying family. For the traveling adult worn out by trip preparations, it might be more aptly called the Sanity Kit! It can begin as a bag of small games, toys, and materials for creative play. After the sojourn, set the collection aside till the next trip so the games and toys within still have new appeal. Add more new ideas for each journey. The kit will grow from year to year as you repack it with old favorites, discard outgrown or used-up parts, and supplement with fresh items to suit the expanding interests and abilities of the children.

Make sure that you choose a bag that is easy to carry, handy to get into, and extremely durable. It is going to see lots of use and hard wear. In helping the children pack their own bags, you will have suggested a balanced selection of items. The same holds true in choosing for the *Surprise Kit*. Look over the lists of suggestions (pp. 188–190). Materials included should offer activity for the variety of ages involved; use of many different skills particularly appropriate and appealing to the group; and a balance of quiet and more active ideas for pacing the trip.

For preschoolers or nonreaders nothing beats the success of story tapes bought from the toy store or borrowed from the library. They come with attractive books included so the children can follow along as the story is told. Mom and Dad have a blissful rest period while the tape recorder does some quiet-time entertaining. A note of caution, however. Beware of the tape that becomes an instant favorite. You may hear it one hundred and fifty times! One parent we know hopes never to hear *Stone Soup ever, ever* again! Choose stories you think might wear well.

A blank tape tucked in can provide a hefty measure of fun for all. The family can become a singing group and do some of its own recording. A couple of family members can write a skit and then produce it on tape. Tape is great for working off frustration in close quarters, too. After a fight with his brother, an eight-year-old we know withdrew deep into his sleeping bag with the tape recorder. Muffled sounds could be heard for a period of time. When he emerged with a wicked glint in his eye, he did a playback of his efforts—a musical ditty with a refrain that went, "I ha-a-a-te my brother!" The grumpy family group broke up with hilarity.

The kind of activity that can last throughout the entire trip provides a continuing thread of interest. One seven-year-old boy who travels the same six-hour route eight times a year always uses a grocery counter to add up the eighteen-wheeler trucks he sees each time along the way. Like the grocery counter, carefully chosen crafts supply prolonged interest and can be picked up and put down at will. *Pom-Pom Making* (p. 33) and *Cross-Stitch on Gingham* (p. 177) are good examples.

Other favorites are masking tape for sticking easily removed patterns and words to windows or back of the seat. Cards are popular standbys for tricks and games.

Wherever you are going—an historical place of interest, a National Park, Disney World, the mountains or seashore, some of your kit choices can be built around learning more about your destination. A packet of maps and pamphlets along with a book or two can heighten interest. The same items pulled out on the return trip will mean even more. While you are at your destination, pick out a coloring book, game, or trinket that pertains to the place and tuck it into your surprise supply for going home.

The idea is to stretch the pulling out of surprises over long periods. You might make up rules to determine when the next item will come out of the bag. Ideas might be: "When we next see a dog." "After the next gas fill up." "When you have all had twenty minutes' quiet time." "When we have had thirty fight-free minutes."

You are in charge of the handouts from your surprise bag. How you pace them will make a great deal of difference in your travel day. Dice from *Dice Decide* (p. 168) pulled out at the right time may break up a fight over who will pay the next toll. The jump rope given just before a rest stop will mean tight muscles can be well exercised before the next lap of the journey. A book for an older child during the preschooler's naptime means a restful period for every-

one. Make sure there is time for rest, time for moving, time for snacking, time for play, all in good balance.

Many of the ideas for car travel adapt well to a train trip. Draw from them next time you go by rail. An airplane, however, does work out a little differently. Most trips by air are amply broken up with snack and meal interruptions. In addition, airlines supply their own entertainment kits for young children. Cards are often available on request. When you take along kit entertainments, choose fewer in number and consider that the space is even more limited than in the car. If you have the misfortune of being stacked up in the air or redirected to another airport, you will be grateful for your own supply to help time pass. It is at just those times when the plane is out of food and entertainment that the flight attendants are a little thin on helpfulness with the kids.

On occasion you and the children will be staying at home, but waving someone else off on a trip. This is a gift-making opportunity for wishing them a good journey. The *Mini Sewing Kit* (p. 180) would be a perfect way for the children to say bon voyage to Grandma, the *Mini Emergency Kit* (p. 184) a fun good-bye to a friend headed for camp, and the *New Neighbor Get-Acquainted Kit* (p. 179) an original welcome for folks who have just you.

A wide range of day trips are a part of our lives. Excursions can mean driving by car or bus to a spot for hiking, swimming, or skiing. Some other objectives might be sightseeing, viewing a ball game, or picking fruits and vegetables.

Day trips require some of the same kinds of planning as longer trips but on a smaller scale. Fewer entertainments are necessary, but you will still want to tuck a few items in a bag to help make time go more quickly and smoothly along the way.

Planning something especially suited to the outing might be fun. A collection of brochures to examine on the way to an historical site or a book on native fish and their habits to pore over while heading for a day of fishing are examples of fitting an activity to the occasion.

A class, playgroup, or scouts will enjoy preplanning their own travel pastimes. Simple games thought out ahead of time and contributions of small pocket toys could cut down on some of the rowdyism sometimes associated with group travels.

Anticipation of the day's plans usually will keep spirits high while you are headed toward the destination, but returning home can be the most trying time. The children are generally exhausted and the fighting begins. Adults themselves often feel too tired to cope. This is the time to pull out a few music and story tape cassettes hidden at the bottom of a surprise bag. Listening activities coupled with the comfort of pillows for sleepy heads can mean a happy, quiet windup for a busy day.

Many outings are short, simple necessities of life. Appointments, carpools, meetings, lessons, and traffic jams are all times when going places means tedium. An older child may wait out the time with an interesting book, or he might carry along a project such as Cross-Stitch on Gingham (p. 177) or Pom-Poms (p. 33) that is easy to pick up and lay down. Keeping a younger child occupied takes imagination. A preschooler might have a special purse containing appealing small toys, games, and knickknacks (p. 170). The contents could be changed from time to time.

Pop a String a Snack (p. 170) into a bag to take. Store a small supply of emergency entertainments in the glove compartment, perhaps a deck of cards so an older child can teach a younger child how to play Black and Red (p. 168) or Snap. Have a brainstorm bag (p. 5) containing two or three unrelated items and see how many things the children can devise to do with them. Keep one or two things stashed in your own purse, perhaps magnets for testing on different surfaces, or a small magnifying glass for examining the surrounding territory. Be ready to invent ridiculous games like Silly Sandwich—"You add ice cream, I'll add a pickle." Remember that young children can be very disconcerted by unfamiliar surroundings. A favorite toy to play with or a familiar activity like sewing cards (p.144) to work at are good choices to carry along.

Going places with children challenges the imagination. The things that happen along the way will be as much a part of the memories as the destination itself. There are so many ways to make any outing a source of pleasure. Test just a few of the ideas given here when you are on the go.

An asterisk next to an item listed in a kit's "materials" section indicates that the item is common to most homes and need not be included in the kit package.

Quick Kits for Going Places

Rub-On Fantasy

Ages 6 and up

Materials

2 rub-on, dry transfer pictures *very* different from one another, for example: dinosaurs and the landing of the *Mayflower.*

Directions

1. Make an imaginary scene on one background using figures from both rub-on pictures.
2. Use your imagination and create the wildest scene that you can.

Stencil Art

Ages 5 and up

Materials

colored pencils
pad of paper
choice of one or two:
letter stencils
templates
picture stencils
shape stencils

Directions

1. Create pictures, words, designs, signs with your selection of stencils and pencils.

Dice Decide

All ages

Materials
pair of dice

Directions
1. Roll dice to see:
   who gets doubles first,
   who gets a die with 6 on it first,
   who gets a throw that adds up to 11 first.
   Think up other numbers to try for!
2. On a trip, use the dice to decide who will get to sit up front, eat the last cookie, or choose the next tape. The dice will be your referee!

Microphone Play

Ages 3 and up

Materials
juice can
dowel rod or stick
tape
string

Directions
1. Tape stick to side of juice can.
2. Tie string to end of the stick for a power line.
3. Be a roving news reporter.

Black and Red Cards

All ages

Materials
a deck of cards (it need not be a complete deck!)

Directions
1. Turn the deck facedown.
2. The first player must guess "black" or "red," then pick up a card. If his guess is wrong, he must put it back into the deck.
3. Let everyone take turns till the pile is gone. See how many cards you can "win."

Jump Rope and Jingle Book

Ages 6 and up

Materials

book of jingles (*Jumprope,* by Peter Skolnik, Workman's Press)

jump rope

Directions

1. Memorize a few verses.
2. Use the rope to practice jumping to verses at your next roadside stop.

Listen!

Ages 4 and up

Materials

tape recorder (on loan)

Choose one or more:

blank tape

story cassettes with book (found at discount, department stores, and record shops)

Guessing Sounds cassette (p. 137)

library cassettes in an assortment of stories, sound tracks, and travel guides

Directions

1. Listen and record en route and during your stay in a motel.

Book Countdown

Ages 3 and up

Materials

library, borrowed or recycled storybooks appropriate for age of receiver

paper to wrap each book (comics are fine)

scotch tape

marker to number each wrapped book

Directions

1. Use for counting the days till parents return home from a trip, or a period in bed comes to an end.
2. Open one a day from the highest number down—10, 9, 8, etc.

String a Snack

Ages 3 and up

Materials

necklace-length piece of string, heavy thread, or dental floss

darning needle

choice of ingredients in sandwich bags:

Cheerios

Fruit Loops

raisins

tiny marshmallows

seedless grapes

napkins

shoe-box to hold all

Directions

1. Dump some of the snacks into the shoe-box lid for easy selection.
2. String snacks with needle and thread (or string). Nibble while you work!
3. Tie your finished work into a snack necklace.

Preschooler's Purse

Ages 2 and up

Materials

old purse

small play items such as:

grocery counter (small manual adding machine)

mirror

small flashlight

comb

cast-off jewelry

inexpensive sunglasses

Directions

1. Turn in your purse now and then for changes and additions to the contents!

Unlock!

Ages 6 and up

Materials

combination lock

math clues for finding the combination such as:

first number of combo is 3 plus 4

second number is 9 minus 1 plus 3

increase difficulty of clues for older children

Directions

1. Use the math clues to open the lock!
2. Make up new clues and try the "unlock" game on a friend.

Pretend Binoculars

Ages 3 and up

Materials

2 empty toilet tissue tubes

small amount of masking tape

shoelace or string cut to necklace length

*hole punch

*scissors

Directions

1. Place paper tubes side by side and tape together firmly.
2. Punch two matching holes at the top end on each side of the binoculars.
3. Attach shoelace or string for neck strap.
4. Peer through your binoculars for a closer look at travel sights.

Activity Kits for Going Places

Color Tester Kit

See what makes colors change.

Ages 4–7

Skills
1. experimentation
2. perception
3. recognition of colors

When
1. while traveling
2. sick in bed activity
3. learning colors with a group

How
1. Have an older child make his own set of color testers and then duplicate materials in a kit for a younger brother, sister, or friend to complete.
2. Prepare kit in advance ready to do for a playgroup outing.

Materials
For making:
   plastic notebook sheet protectors
   cellophane in primary colors: red, blue, yellow
   *scissors
   transparent tape
For packaging and directions:
   manila envelope

Assembling
1. Cut plastic page crosswise into 3 equal pieces.
2. Write directions on the envelope.
3. Tuck all materials into the envelope.

Directions for Color Tester Kit
1. Cut a piece of cellophane to fit inside a plastic piece.
2. Slip the cellophane into the plastic insert piece. Repeat with other cellophane colors.
3. Close openings in plastic by taping.
4. Hold your color testers up to the light in front of one another in different combinations and see what new colors can be made!

Autograph Clipboard Kit

A practical gift made exciting with a collection of autographs.

Ages 6 and up

Skills
1. artistic expression
2. originality
3. socialization

When
1. moving-away gift
2. car activity
3. visit-a-friend gift
4. reward for excellent school report

How
1. A small group might jointly decorate and autograph a clipboard to give a friend who is moving away.
2. Some children enjoy assembling the makings of two clipboards for project sharing with a friend.
3. For use in the car, prepaint the board and give with markers for an en route decorating project.
4. Group leaders can adapt this for a neat decoupage project.

Materials
For making:
    plain clipboard (any size)
    white latex or acrylic paint (use what you have on hand)
    paintbrush
    set of permanent magic markers

optional: new pencil or pen
    pad of paper or stationery
    clear spray
For packaging:
    gift box
    wrapping to suit the occasion
For directions:
    greeting card

Assembling
1. Write directions on a greeting card and clamp to the board.
2. Place clipboard, decorating supplies, and optional materials into the box.
3. Wrap appropriately.

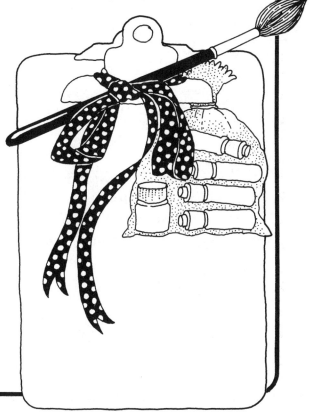

Directions for Autograph Clipboard Kit

1. Paint the board. Let dry. Add a second coat if necessary.
2. Use the markers to personalize your clipboard with your name and an original design.
3. Have friends autograph the board. Optional: Spray with clear finish.
4. Enjoy using your board for *Clipboard Pencil and Paper Games* (p.191).
5. Copy this kit idea for gift giving to friends of all ages.

Berry-Picking Basket Kit

Give a berry-picking outing a touch of glamour!

Ages 6 and up

Skills
1. making selections
2. cutting and gluing
3. combining materials to create designs

When
1. readying for a berry-picking trip
2. a party favor for berry-picking birthday celebration
3. surprise gift to welcome summer
4. hostess gift for berry lover (filled with blueberry muffins)

How
1. A child can use baskets as unique invitations for friends to come along on a berry-picking outing. Complete one for each guest, personalize with guest's name, and label with date, time, and place; OR give each person *the makings* for a basket. Include information about the upcoming spree.
2. Adapt the basket idea to other pick-your-own produce outings.
3. Adults might use the basket as a gift in exchange for favorite blueberry recipes.

Materials
For making:

new, unused paint-mixing buckets, empty quart-size ice cream containers, or wooden oval mushroom baskets (from food exchange or grocery store)

*hole punch

string or braided yarn

decorating materials:

  combine or use separately:

    permanent magic markers

    acrylic paint, brush, water dish

    pages from gardening magazines

  Mod Podge sealer (hobby shops) or any clear finish

    *scissors, glue

    ¾ ″ sponge brush

  optional: a few favorite recipes for berries

For packaging:

  the basket

  brown bag

  yarn

For directions:

  recipe file card with fruit sticker or magazine picture to decorate

Assembling

1. Write directions on the outside of the brown bag.
2. Tuck recipes and basket full of materials into the brown bag.
3. Punch 2 holes in the folded bag top and tie with yarn.

Directions for Berry-Picking Basket Kit

1. GET READY FOR BERRY PICKING!
2. Decorate your picking box with a berry-picking theme. Cut and paste, paint, draw, or use marker. Put your name on the box for a special touch. Be careful not to decorate the inside. Berry stains are the only safe design for inside the food basket!
3. For professional finish, coat decorated container with Mod Podge. Allow to dry.
4. Punch a hole on opposite sides of your box. Tie string or braided yarn on for neck strap.

Please join us for berry picking on Saturday!

Grandma Stoklosa's Cookie Mix

Young cooks bake travel treats.

Ages 7 to adult

Skills
1. measuring, cooking
2. following directions
3. recognizing equivalents

When
1. bake to take on a trip
2. welcome gift for new family
3. to use with baby-sitter
4. indoor day activity

How
1. An older child, baby-sitter, or adult will enjoy giving the mix to a young friend. A time for sharing the baking session can be arranged.
2. A more complete cook's kit can be made by adding a new cookie sheet, spatula, or apron.

Materials
For making:
    wooden spoon
    *large mixing bowl
    *measuring and other utensils
    recipe makes 2 mix kits:
        3 cups powdered milk
        2½ cups flour
        1 teaspoon baking soda
        1¼ teaspoons salt
        1 cup granulated sugar
        1 cup brown sugar
        1½ cups solid shortening
        3½ cups quick oats
        1 cup chocolate bits
        1 cup raisins
    (water, egg, vanilla to be added later, see recipe directions)
For packaging:
    airtight plastic containers or plastic bags and twist 'ems
    colorful ribbon
For directions:
    recipe card

Assembling
1. Method for mix recipe: Mix first six ingredients. Cut in shortening until blended. Stir in oats thoroughly. Add raisins and chocolate chips. Halve the mixture and store in airtight containers or closed bags. Mix may be stored in the refrigerator for several weeks.
2. Write recipe card. Include the necessary ingredients for making the mix *and* directions for completing and baking.
3. Attach card to mix with pretty bow.

Directions for Grandma Stoklosa's Cookie Mix Kit

1. Empty one bag of mix into a bowl.
2. With a wooden spoon make a "hole" in the mix and put into it 1 egg, ⅓ cup water, and ½ teaspoon vanilla.
3. Mix well.
4. Drop by teaspoonsful onto ungreased cookie sheet.
5. Bake at 350° F. for 12 to 15 minutes. Makes about 4½ dozen cookies.

Cross-Stitch on Gingham Kit

Gingham squares make built-in guidelines for beginning stitchery!

Ages 8 and up

Skills

1. perceptual planning
2. counting
3. precision

When

1. travel
2. continuing project at home
3. sick in bed
4. birthday gift

How

1. This kit might be given by one child to another with an invitation to start the project together on a specified date.
2. This project is great to do alone, with a friend, or while Mom sews!

Materials

For making:

large scraps of gingham
embroidery hoop
embroidery floss in several colors
embroidery needle
*scissors
For packaging:
bag with handles or drawstring, or
small basket with handle
optional: gift wrapping
For directions:
pad of graph paper

Assembling

1. Sew a few sample designs or letters on gingham. Draw sample letters and designs on graph paper.
2. Write directions on the graph paper beneath the drawings.
3. Wrap materials individually if you wish. Arrange everything in basket or bag with directions.
4. For extra fun, include an invitation with special time stated for starting a project with the child.

Directions for Cross-Stitch on Gingham Kit

1. Fit your fabric onto the embroidery hoop, and practice copying the patterns already done on the gingham sample, or on the graph paper.

2. Helpful sewing hints: Tie floss through eye of needle so it will not become unthreaded. Knot the end slightly. Keep your floss 12″ long. Work your needle from opposite corners of each gingham square to be stitched.

3. In stores look for items that are made from gingham, such as dish towels, aprons, a blouse. Cross-stitch initials or names on your purchases. What great gifts to give!

New Neighbor Get-Acquainted Kit

A surprise to make new folks feel welcome!

All ages

Skills

1. discovery
2. reference
3. map reading
4. logical planning

When

1. a new family or person moves into the area
2. family fun for a day off from school and work
3. a birthday party outing

How

1. Adult or older child can do the assembling of materials. The whole family can help plan what things the new neighbors might most like to explore.
2. When used as a birthday party idea, give a kit to each guest as a party favor.

Materials

For doing:

Choose an assortment; keeping in mind the ages and possible interests of the new family.
bus, train, subway schedules
list of things to explore first with favorite places starred
map of the area with starting point and key spots of interest circled
pamphlets or brochures from places such as museums, zoo, points of historical interest
folder with pockets
calendar with upcoming events marked on the date (include when possible a chance to enjoy an event together)

For packaging:
wrapping (a road map would be interesting)
ribbon

For directions:
a welcome card

Assembling

1. Slip maps, brochures, etc., into pockets of folder.
2. Wrap and attach welcome card with directions.
3. Deliver, perhaps accompanied by some special bread or coffee cake.

Directions for New Neighbor Get-Acquainted Kit

Sample card:

Welcome to our area! Use the enclosed to explore your new surroundings. Call us for extra suggestions.

Mini Sewing Kit

Fun to make and handy to use.

Ages 8 and up

Skills
1. eye-hand coordination
2. reading and following directions
3. manipulation

When
1. going-away surprise
2. small group gift-making project
3. thank-you for teacher
4. stocking stuffer
5. sick-in-bed project

How
1. Speed up draggy pretrip waiting time. Give this to a restless child to make for the upcoming vacation.

Materials
For making:
    2 spools of thread
    2 small matching plastic lids (from cheese or margarine tubs)
    12″ yarn scrap
    2½″ × 5″ piece felt or other heavy fabric
    pins and needles
    nail, hole punch, or pointed scissors
For packaging:
    plastic sandwich bag
    yarn scrap
    envelope
For directions:
    file card or homemade colored paper card

Assembling
1. Seal pins and needles in envelope.
2. Tuck all materials into sandwich bag.
3. Write directions onto card.
4. With yarn, tie bag shut and attach directions.

Directions for Mini Sewing Kit

1. Stand the two spools of thread side by side. Measure distance between center holes of the spools.

2. Use nail, paper punch, or scissors to punch holes in each plastic lid the same distance apart as spool holes.

3. Make a sandwich with the spools of thread between the lids.

4. Thread yarn through the holes in the lids and spools to hold the "sandwich" together. Tie yarn in bow on the top.

5. Fold fabric in half like book and punch hole in top left corner. Attach to yarn bow.

6. Stick pin and needle supply into sides of fabric "book."

Battleship Game Kit

An old favorite minus toymakers' plastic frills!

Ages 8 and up

Skills
1. concentration
2. reasoning and logical thinking
3. writing
4. competition

When
1. car trips
2. waiting rooms
3. confined to bed

How
1. An adult who has access to a copying machine can draw a master sheet and run off a stack of copies for a gift surprise, party favors, or classroom enrichment activity.

Materials
For making:
    pad of ¼″ graph paper
    2 pencils
    2 6-inch rulers
For packaging and directions:
    brown mailing envelope
    gift wrapping

Assembling
1. Draw sample sheet and tape to one side of the envelope. Directions for sample:

a. Draw a box measuring 10 squares by 10 squares at the top of the page. Repeat at the bottom of the page.

b. Number over each box in the top line across 1–10. Letter beside each square in the first vertical line, A-J. Repeat in the box below.

c. Label the top box MINE; the bottom box, THE ENEMY. Draw a sample "battleship" in the box marked MINE by outlining five squares that go in a straight line, up and down or across. It can be anywhere. Do the same for the "cruiser," four squares; "destroyer," three squares; and "submarine," two squares. Label kinds of ships.

d. Print playing directions on the other side of the envelope. Put materials inside.

2. Gift wrap if you wish.

Directions for Battleship Game Kit

Two players:

1. Copy from the sample sheet. In the MINE box "hide" your ships in different places.

2. Give THE ENEMY a chance to hit your ships. He may say "A3." You put an x in your box in square A3. If it hits one of your ships, you must tell your opponent he has a hit. He will outline square A3 in his ENEMY box.

3. Now it is your turn. Maybe you say "B4." If he tells you you have a hit, outline box B4. You will know that you should hit up and down, to the right or left of this box, until you "sink" one of his ships.

4. Take turns until someone's ships have all been sunk.

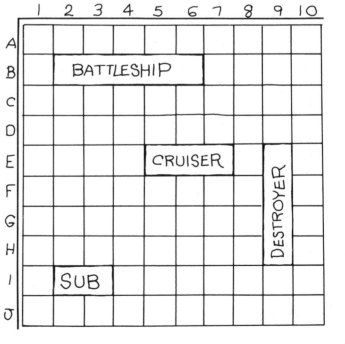

Mini Emergency Kit

Off on some adventure? Be prepared for ANYTHING!

Ages 7 and up

Skills
1. concern for the unexpected
2. evaluating needs
3. safety

When
1. to take on a trip
2. scout project
3. going-away gift
4. stocking stuffer

How
1. Group leaders will find this an excellent project to do in preparation for hike or field trip.
2. Grandparents will find this a quick but satisfying activity to share with the younger generation.

Materials
For making:
  hole punch or nail
  plastic film container with lid (free from photo stores)
  string
  Band-Aid ™
  dime for emergency call
  needle
  scrap of soap
For packaging:
  plastic sandwich bag
  twist 'em or ribbon
For directions:
  file card decorated with red cross or glued-on Band-Aid

Assembling
1. Write directions on card. Label it MINI EMERGENCY KIT.
2. Toss materials into bag and tie shut.
3. Attach direction card.

Directions for Mini Emergency Kit
1. Get ready for splinters, cuts, and calling for help!
2. With hole punch or nail, punch hole in the center of the lid.
3. Loop string around your neck and thread ends through lid hole. Make a large knot inside to hold. You may need to double-knot the string.
4. Insert needle point in soap piece.
5. Place all items in tube and snap to lid.

Collection Starter Kit

Trip trivia leads to collecting fun!

For all ages

Skills
1. developing new interests
2. logical planning
3. making comparisons

When
1. on a trip
2. sick in bed
3. rainy day

How
1. Traveling parents or grandparents can start a child on his collection and add to it as they come back from other trips.
2. A day's trip to the city or an extended vacation trip gives a child a chance to pick up additions.

Materials
For making:

Choose one of these categories for collection:
> bottle caps
> patches
> matchbook covers (matches removed)
> stamps
> postcards
> patches
> coins
> beer cans
> brochures

scrapbook or poster board

flat cardboard boxes for rocks or beer cans (at places where soda is sold)

white glue

For packaging:
> box
> wrapping

For directions:
> postcard or construction paper tag with a matchbook cover, bottle cap or other collectibles glued on

Assembling
1. Put all materials in box and wrap. Attach directions.
2. Poster board can be rolled and taped or rubber banded.

Directions for Collection Starter Kit
1. Sort the items you are collecting.
2. Glue them in a book or mount them on posters or in a box to display.
3. Trade with friends.
4. Look for ways to continue your collection and expand it.

Explore Grab Bag Kit

"Extras" that add to the enjoyment of a trip.

Ages 7 and up

Skills

1. observation
2. reference
3. reading
4. recording

When

1. on a long trip
2. camping-out vacation
3. walk in the woods or at the seashore
4. house gift when visiting friends' vacation home

How

1. The making of collecting pail and scoop can be a pretrip project.
2. Books can be wrapped and used as treats to enjoy during the journey or in anticipation of the vacation.

Materials

For making of collecting pail and scoop:
  2 empty plastic bleach containers
  piece of cord
  *sharp, pointed scissors
  *punch
For nature projects and identification:
  identification books (shells, rocks, wildflowers, birds, stars)
  felt pen
  self-sticking labels
  notebook or special travel log
For quiet moments: (in anticipation of, during, or following the trip)
  Paperback books with a story or theme appropriate for the place where the travelers are going. A cookbook might be fun for seafood or campfire cookery. Examples for those headed to the seashore:

  Captain Goody Books, published by Chatham Press (Cape Cod)
  Moominpappa Goes to Sea, by Tove Jansson, published by Camelot Books/Avon
  Adventure at Black Rock Cave, by Lauber, published by Scholastic Book Services
  The Beachcombers Book, by Bernice Kohn, published by Viking
  When the Tide Goes Out, by Waddell, published by World Publishing Co.
  Or if you are headed to northern U.S. or Canada around the Great Lakes region: *Paddle to the Sea,*

by Holling, published by Houghton Mifflin Co.

Add your own reference and reading ideas to the kit. A coloring book with the appropriate theme for preschoolers, a native recipe book for the gourmet, and fishing tackle and information for the sportsman.

For packaging and directions:

drawstring bag, cloth or plastic ribbon

greeting or notecard with appropriate theme

Assembling

1. Wrap items individually and place in drawstring bag.
2. Tie with a bow.
3. Attach card with directions.

Directions for Explore Grab Bag Kit

1. Make a pail and scoop

   Pail: Cut off upper part of plastic bottle, even the handle. Punch holes on opposite sides and tie on a cord handle.

   Scoop: Leave the handle on the plastic bottle. Hold the bottle on its side and cut a piece diagonally from the bottom to leave a large opening for scooping.

   Use to gather materials native to the seashore, mountains, and lakes.

2. Label findings like shells, rocks, etc. Use nature identification books to help.

3. Read a gift book on a rainy day, or read little bits of it aloud each night with other members of the family or group. Sharing aloud is the most fun and can even be done en route in the car.

4. Keep a travel log. Tell where and how you gathered your "finds." Make note of weather and changes around you like an especially high tide, snow at the top of the mountain, or bear tracks at the campsite.

Going Places Surprise Kit

Tried and true inexpensive entertainments found at local stores.

Ages 3 and up

Skills varied according to kit contents

When
1. long car trips
2. family camping trips
3. get-well gifts
4. stocking stuffers and Easter basket fillers
5. small rewards and surprises
6. gifts for any occasion

How
1. Assemble a travel surprise kit for each child according to his age and interests. Balance the contents: something to do alone, with someone, paper project, small toy, something for quiet, something aloud, a game, art, something to run off energy at a stop!
2. Space the giving of the gifts. Promise one after a certain time lapse (½ hour) or when you have gone 40 miles. Eager children watch the clock and odometer. Use gift giving as rewards for no fighting for 15 minutes or after everyone has had a 20-minute quiet time.
3. Anyone can use the list of materials here as an aid for making handy gift shopping lists.
4. Parents can enlist the help of children to assemble travel activity kits before a vacation. Youngsters become happily involved when waiting is hard and mother is busy.
5. A family will enjoy assembling a gift kit of their favorite travel pastimes to give friends who regularly travel on weekends.

Materials (choose a balanced variety)
Note: Check age suggestions beside each list. Your child's age may be included in two or more.
For children *3 and up*:
  Choose:
    crayons
    colored paper
    pad of paper
    pencil
    carbon paper
    puppets
    clipboard
    flashlight
    color forms
    puzzles
    small stack boxes
    set of small blocks
    order book with carbon
    superheroes
    small dolls

magic writing board (lift up page and writing disappears)

miniature toys (car, plane, wiggly monsters, or animals)

large ball (for use during roadside stops)

library books or paperback stories

cassettes (stories, sing-along music, favorite pieces from library)

blank cassette (record your own singing, stories, or diary of trip adventures)

For children *4 and up:*
  Choose:
    loose leaf or spiral notebook
    scrapbook
    glue stick
    blunt scissors
    sticker book
    stamp sponge
    peel and stick geometric shapes
    block puzzles (small set of 6 blocks)
    magnetic puzzles
    auto bingo
    drawing keyboard (plastic board containing black substance, key smoothes the black, then is used to draw so colors beneath are revealed.)

For children *5 and up:*
  Choose:
    dice
    chalk (white and colored)
    small blackboard and dampened sponge

hole punch

magnetic games

tape (scotch for fastening, colored to make designs, masking for games and art)

large-sized deck of cards (Old Maid, Fish, etc.)

small marionettes with few strings

frisbee (use during stops)

stickers (stars, pictures, letters)

stencils or templates (animals, geometric shapes)

punch-out pictures and books

pocket games (Tomy's excellent)

For children *6 and up:*
  Choose:
    felt pens (various colors, widths)
    autograph book
    pencils
    novelty erasers
    hand pencil sharpener
    sticky-backed colored paper
    magnetic checkers
    combination lock
    jump rope (use at stops)
    string for Cat's Cradle
    individual Lego Kits (truck, car)
    children's game decks of cards
    peel and stick letters
    protractor
    stencils or templates (letters, various curves and shapes)
    magic pad (scribbling over page surface with pencil makes picture appear)
    rub-ons or dry pressure transfers

(letters, numbers, pictures transferred to paper or other surface by rubbing with edge of coin or pencil) (*Rub-on Fantasy,* p. 167).

Doodle Board (magnetic rod used to pick up metal beads to make designs and pictures)

For packaging and directions:

drawstring plastic bag, shopping bag with handles, beach bag with pockets, knitting bag, insulated picnic bag, or small duffel bag

small paper or plastic bags

optional: gift wrapping for each gift

Assembling

1. Put items that seem to "go together" to make an activity into smaller bags or individual wrappings. For example, stencil, paper, pencil, or crayons (*Stencil Art,* p. 167).

2. Write directions or activity suggestions on the bags or wrapping. Use your imagination to suggest activity as with peel and stick letters: "Stick messages on the window near you! Put a message or two on the back of a seat."

3. Include directions for one or two "out loud" games (*pencil and paper games* p. 191).

4. Number the packages for order of giving, if you wish.

5. Place all gifts in big bag and label SURPRISE KIT. Write any additional directions on the outside.

Directions for Going Places Surprise Kit

1. Carefully read the directions for each gift in the kit.

2. Try your own brainstorm ideas using the same materials.

3. Enjoy your trip!

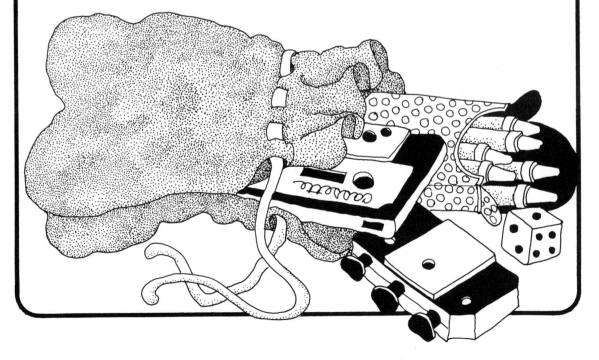

Clipboard Pencil and Paper Games Kit

Fun to play as you are on the go or vacation bound!

Ages (see each game)

Skills
1. writing
2. following directions
3. making selections

When
1. on-the-way trip activity
2. rainy day at the beach or camping out
3. bon voyage gift
4. sick in bed
5. spare-time activities for a group
6. by the fireside

How
1. Xeroxing directly from the book or typing are the quickest ways to put together game rules for this kit.
2. Each time you pack for a trip, include the clipboard with a new selection of pencil and paper games.

Materials
For making:
   clipboard
   pad of plain paper
   colored pencils or markers
   game rules
   Choice of inexpensive purchased activities:
      coloring books (related to itinerary)
      Kenner's Yes and No Game Books
      hidden picture books
      crossword puzzles
      math puzzles
      mazes
      Mad libs
      dot to dot (ages 5–7)
For packaging and directions:
   manila envelope
   business envelope
   file cards or paper
   optional: parts of a map, picture of a car, train, plane, etc., to glue to the manila envelope for a travel theme decoration.

Assembling
1. Make a selection of games and copy the rules on file cards or paper. Put into business envelope. Include some of your own favorites. *Battleship* (p. 182) is a good starting suggestion.
2. Write directions on outside of manila envelope.
3. Put rules and game materials into manila envelope. Make sure you include special game items needed to play each game.
4. Clip packaged selection to clipboard.

Directions for Clipboard Pencil and Paper Games Kit

Pencil and Paper Games for more than one person:

1. Choose a game rule card. Clip it with a large sheet of paper to your board. Play! Then enjoy some of the other game surprises.

Dot to Dot ages 6 and up
  Directions:
1. Prepare a paper with even rows of equal numbers of dots. (peg board makes perfect stencil)
2. Take turns drawing horizontal or vertical lines between any two dots. Each player should use a different color pencil.
3. Try to prevent your opponents from completing a box.
4. When you complete a box, write your initials inside.
5. The winner is the person who completes the greatest number of boxes.

Circle the Number (p. 121) *ages 4 and up*
Treasure Hunt ages 3 and up
  Directions:
1. Make lists in sets of twelve, naming sights most often seen in cities or towns. You might use simple pictures for the nonreaders in the group.
2. Sample listing: flag, mail truck, chimney with smoke, U-Haul truck, fire alarm box, dog on leash, empty building, road construction, brick house.
   Make up new lists as you collect ideas in your travels. Add seasonal items such as pumpkin, sprinkler, snowman, etc.
3. Read the list aloud to the nonreaders in the car. Everyone look for the items on the first list. The winner is the first to find 10 of the objects on the list. Try another list.
4. You can divide up your group and play in teams. See if you can replay the same list and find more sights in less time! Work together and try to better your records from the last city or town.

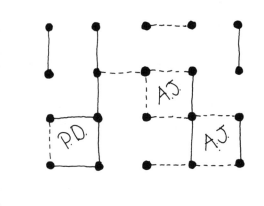

See the United States ages 8 and up
  Directions:
1. Make a list of the 50 states in alphabetical order.
2. Look for license plates from each state. Check off the ones you find in your travels. Look for ones you have not seen.
3. Keep this list in the car so it becomes a continuing activity during a long trip or on shorter outings throughout the year.

Sign Countdown ages 7 and up
  Directions:
1. Each player will need to make a list of advertising signs he or she expects to see on buildings, vehicles, or billboards.
2. Each person looks for the signs on his own list.
3. The winner is the one who finds the most.

Spelling Ghost ages 8 and up
  Directions:
1. Let one player begin a word with a single letter. Have the next player add another.
2. Have each player take turns adding one letter to the beginning or end of the group of letters. Each player will need to have a real word in his mind.
3. Try *not* to complete a word on your turn.
4. Each time you do complete a word you are given a letter from the word "ghost."
5. The winner is the last person to become "G-H-O-S-T!"

Word Match ages 9 and up
  Directions:
1. Write down separate lists of synonyms, antonyms, and homonyms. Include as many as you can think of to list. Samples for using to start:
   synonym (means the same) big-large, thin-skinny
   antonym (means the opposite) hot-cold, high-low
   homonym (sounds the same but means something different) red-read, right-write
2. The winner is the person with the longest list!

Word Puzzle Luck ages 8 and up
Directions:
1. On paper make several rows of letters. Make sure you have the same number of letters in each row and that they line up neatly under one another. One third of the letters in each row should be vowels.
2. Take turns circling words made from letters that sit next to one another. The words may be read from left to right, backward, up and down, or on the diagonal.
3. Each player should use a different color pencil, then it will be easy to count how many words "belong" to each player! The person with the most words is the winner.

Pencil and Paper Games for someone to play alone:

Create Codes ages 6 and up
Directions:
1. Dream up code system all your own.
2. Write out a message in your code and see who will be the first to figure it out.

Graph Paper Designs ages 5 and up
Special Materials:
graph paper
Directions:
1. Use all markers available.
2. Color in the blocks to form abstract patterns or block letters.

Postcard Writing ages 6 and up
Special Materials:
trip postcards
Directions:
1. Promise a post office stop after 6 postcards have been written.
2. An excuse for an exercise stop will encourage children to write.

Squiggle Drawings (p. 136) ages 5 and up

Thumb and Fingerprint Doodles (p. 35) ages 5 and up

Travel Diary ages 7 and up
Special Materials:
notebook or diary
Directions:
1. Jot down what occurs during the day. At night go over the list and write about the day's adventures in your diary.
2. Preschoolers enjoy drawing what especially interests them along the way. Adults may later help them label.

Appendix I

Activities by Type

Arts and Crafts

ACTIVITY OR RECIPE BOX, 14, 102

AUTOGRAPH CLIPBOARD, 130, 173

Bag of Clay, 96, 132

BAG-OF-LABELS MAKE-A-GAME, 25, 50

baskets, 97, 174

BATTLESHIP, 4, 164, 182, 191

BERRY-PICKING BASKET, 174

BIG-MOUTH DISGUISE, 70, 94

box activities, 70, 75, 102, 116, 140

brainstorm list, 5, 26, 166

clay, 96, 132

CLOTH FLOWERS, 94, 138

CLOTHESLINE STORY AND DISPLAY, 84

CLOWN, 114

COLLAGE MEMORIES, 103

collections, 9, 153, 185

COLOR TESTERS, 172

costumes, 41, 45, 62, 70, 114, 116

Crayon Rubbings, 135

CROSS-STITCH ON GINGHAM, 130, 165, 166, 177

cut-and-paste activities, 32, 50, 61, 70, 72, 101, 103, 105, 110, 112, 114, 116, 132, 138, 147

cutting; special variations, 61, 103, 110, 112, 138, 147

decorating items, 32, 33, 51, 61, 65, 72, 87, 96, 135, 138, 146, 152

DO-YOUR-THING, 6, 41

dried flowers and weeds, 5, 110

FAMILY BOUQUET, 20, 95, 110, 131

FELT-BOARD TEPEE, 130, 156

FINGERPAINT FUN, 66, 130

fingerpainting, 66, 130

FLASHLIGHT PLANETARIUM, 9, 151

flowers, 69, 100, 110, 138, 142

frames for photos, 103

gift containers, 97, 122, 174, 186

gift kits, 96, 97, 100, 101, 122, 179

gift wrapping, 11–14

gifts (See GIFTS section, Appendix I)

glue (See cut-and-paste activities, magnets, shells)

Heidi's Paper Bag Piñata, 98

Instant Wall Hanging, 65

KITCHEN-MADE SAND ART, 21, 25, 51

Linoleum Block Prints, 14, 27, 164

LOG BIRD FEEDER, 44, 86, 130

MAGNET ART, 32

MAKE YOUR OWN CARDS, 112

May Day Pin Basket, 97

media center, 136, 168, 169

Microphone Play, 168

MINI EMERGENCY KIT, 165, 184

MINI SEWING KIT, 165, 180

MINIATURE SCENE, 7, 94, 140

mixing colors, 172

modeling, 96, 132,

mosaics, 6

MYSTERY FEELY BOX, 75

NEWSPAPER BOAT FOLDING, 121, 158

packaging, 11–14

pails and scoops (*See* EXPLORE GRAB BAG, 186)

painting, 35, 66, 70, 72, 84, 98, 134, 136, 148, 167

PAINTBRUSH COOKIES, 148

paper bag activities, 98, 99

PAPER DOLL SET DESIGN, 94, 147

paper punch, 6

Party Favor Bag, 99

Patchwork Scribbles, 134

PERSONALIZED PENCIL CASE OR BOOK BAG, 105

Photo Album, 132

photos, 103, 110, 132

piñata, 98

ping pong balls, 5

PLANT A DESERT, 142

Playdough Marble Roll Game, 132

POM-POM MAKING, 16, 20, 33, 58, 115, 130, 165, 166

Pretend Binoculars, 149, 171

PRINGLE'S BUG CATCHER, 9, 82, 131

puppets, 7

QUILT-MAKING IRON-ON, 7, 57, 72

RHYTHM ART, 78

ROBOT COSTUME, 116

Rub-on Fantasy, 167

sand, 5, 51

School Photo Bookmark, 101

scrapbooks, 132

scraps, 7

sewing, 33, 72, 144, 177, 180

SEWING CARD, 17, 21, 33, 130, 144, 166

shells, 153

SHELL IDENTIFICATION, 10, 153

SPARKLING WINDOW SHADE PULLS, 7, 93, 130, 146

Squiggle Story Notebook, 136

Stencil Art, 167

straws, 5

String a Snack, 170

strumming instrument, 79

TAPE RESIST GAME BOARD, 15, 88, 119

THUMB AND FINGERPRINT DOODLES, 13, 35, 131, 194

Tissue Paper Stained Glass, 61

Wooden Spoon Boutique Gift, 96

wrapping, 12–13

VEGETABLE SCULPTURES, 16, 25, 26, 28

Cooking

baking, 37, 38, 100, 119, 148, 176

BERRY-PICKING BASKET, 174

BEST EVER COCOA MIX, 58, 67, 119, 122

birthday cake, 100

candy, 106

CANDY HOUSE, 106, 108

cereal, 170

cocoa, 67

COOKIE CUTTER KNOX BLOX, 16, 21, 109

cookies, 37, 148, 176

desserts, 37, 60, 98, 100, 106, 109, 148, 176

drinks, 40, 67

EASY PIZZA MAKING, 20, 26, 38, 94, 119, 131

FIRESIDE KIT, 119

GRANDMA STOKLOSA'S COOKIE MIX, 119, 122, 164, 176

Ice-Cream-Cone Clowns, 98

Instant S'Mores, 60

KITCHEN-MADE SAND ART, 21, 25, 51

M and M PARTY COOKIES, 16, 37, 115, 164

METRIC SNACK, 16, 80

Mystery Smelling Jars, 64

NEW NEIGHBOR GET-ACQUAINTED KIT, 165, 179

PAINTBRUSH COOKIES, 122, 148

pizza, 38

RECIPE BOX, (ACTIVITY OR), 1, 4, 102

ROOT BEER MAKING, 4, 40, 119

salad, 104

Speedy Birthday Cake, 100

SPOOK SALAD-MAKING, 104, 131

String a Snack, 170

VEGETABLE SCULPTURES, 16, 25, 26, 28

Dramatic Play

ACTRESS PRETEND, 52,

ARMY-NAVY CAMP-OUT PRETEND, 45

BIG-MOUTH DISGUISE, 70, 94

brainstorm list, 5, 26, 166

CLOWN, 114

combinations, 3, 5

costumes, 4, 41, 45, 62, 70, 114, 116

DO YOUR THING, 6, 41

FELT-BOARD TEPEE, 130, 156

Halloween, 70, 94, 104, 114, 116

Invisible Ink, 30

Listen!, 169

Microphone Play, 168

MINI EMERGENCY KIT, 165, 184

Mystery Purse, 101

Nothing-to-Do Jar, 29

OLYMPIC GAMES, 57, 90, 130

PAPER DOLL SET DESIGN, 94, 147

ping pong balls, 5

Pretend Binoculars, 171

puppets, 7

Recording, 136, 137, 169

ROBOT COSTUME, 116

Squeeze-Bottle Squirt Play, 29

STRUMMING, 79

tape recording, 136, 137, 169

Tin Can Golf, 29

Weather Bureau, 30

Games

ARMY-NAVY CAMP-OUT PRETEND, 45,

BAG-OF-LABELS MAKE-A-GAME, 25, 50

BATTLESHIP, 4, 164, 182, 191

bean bags, 20

bed basketball, 10

Black and Red Cards, 168

boat-sinking game, 121

Book Countdown, 169

brainstorm list, 5, 26, 166

cards, 112, 168

CLIPBOARD PENCIL AND PAPER GAMES, 119, 130, 174, 190, 191

Color Play, 133

COLOR TESTER, 164, 171

common objects, 5–8

Dice Decide, 168

FELT-BOARD TEPEE, 130, 156

FIRESIDE KIT, 20, 67, 94, 119

FLOOR POOL GAME, 118, 119, 130

FOLLOW THE FOOTSTEPS, 76

game board, 88

GOING-PLACES SURPRISE, 8, 130, 164, 188

GUESS THE SOUNDS AND TUNES, 136, 137, 169

Heidi's Paper Bag Piñata, 98

hockey, indoor, 48

hopscotch, indoor, 48

Jump Rope and Jingle Book, 169

Map Fun, 132

masking tape ideas, 48, 88

MASKING TAPE FLOOR GAMES, 6, 48, 58, 130

MYSTERY FEELY BOX, 75

Mystery Purse, 101

Mystery Smelling Jars, 64

NEWSPAPER BOAT FOLDING, 158

Nothing-to-Do Jar, 29

OLYMPIC GAMES, 57, 90, 130

paper and pencil games, 191

Party Favor Bag, 99

PARTY GAME KIT, 16, 94, 119, 120, 158, 159, 192

party games, 120

penny toss or dropping, 121

ping pong ball, 5

Playdough Marble Roll Game, 132

poster game, 136

Preschooler's Purse, 170

Pup Tent, 28

Ring a Bell, 60

sandbox shell play, 153

Spotlight Game, 136

Squeeze-Bottle Squirt Play, 29

stocking stuffers, 8

straws, 5

TAPE RESIST GAME BOARD, 15, 88, 119

Tin Can Golf, 29

travel games, 168, 169, 170, 171, 182, 186, 188, 191

Work-and-Play Project Board, 135

Unlock!, 171

Gifts

combination gifts, 3, 5

gifts to make:

ACTIVITY OR RECIPE BOX, 14, 102

AUTOGRAPH CLIPBOARD, 130, 173

Bag of Clay, 96

BAG-OF-LABELS MAKE-A-GAME, 25, 50

BATTLESHIP, 4, 164, 182, 191

BERRY-PICKING BASKET, 174

BEST EVER COCOA MAKING, 58, 67, 119, 122

CANDY HOUSE, 106, 108

CLOTH FLOWERS, 94, 138

COLLAGE MEMORIES, 103

Color Tester, 172

CROSS-STITCH ON GINGHAM, 130, 165, 166, 177

FAMILY BOUQUET, 20, 95, 110, 131

FIRESIDE KIT, 20, 67, 94, 119

Flame Color Mix, 99

FELT-BOARD TEPEE, 130, 156

FLASHLIGHT PLANETARIUM, 9, 151

GRANDMA STOKLOSA'S COOKIE MIX, 119, 122, 164, 176

HANG-YOUR-JEWELS HOLDER, 152

Heidi's Paper Bag Piñata, 98

Instant Wall Hanging, 65

KITCHEN-MADE SAND ART, 21, 25, 51

LIGHTEN-YOUR-LOAD HELP, 94, 95, 122

LOG BIRD FEEDER, 44, 86, 130

M and M PARTY COOKIES, 16, 37, 115, 164

MAGNET ART, 32

MAKE YOUR OWN CARDS, 112

May Day Pin Basket, 97

METRIC SNACK, 16, 80

MINI EMERGENCY KIT, 165, 184

MINI SEWING KIT, 165, 180

MYSTERY FEELY BOX, 75

MYSTERY SMELLING JARS, 64

NAPKIN HOLDER, 44, 58, 87

NARCISSUS PLANTING, 69

NEW NEIGHBOR GET-ACQUAINTED KIT, 165, 179

OLYMPIC GAMES, 57, 90, 130

pail and scoop (See EXPLORE GRAB BAG, 186)

PERSONALIZED PENCIL CASE, 105

PLANT A DESERT, 142

Playdough Marble Roll Game, 132

POM-POM MAKING, 16, 20, 33, 58, 115, 130, 165, 166

Pretend Binoculars, 171

QUILT-MAKING IRON-ON, 7, 57, 72

School Photo Book Mark, 101

SPARKLING WINDOW SHADE, PULLS, 7, 93, 130, 146

STOMPERS 'N' STILTS, 123

TAPE RESIST GAME BOARD, 15, 88, 119

Wooden Spoon Boutique Gift, 96

Work-and-Play Project Board, 135

Violet-by-Mail Surprise, 100

in bags, 12–13

in boxes, 12–13

packaging, 11–14

special occasions, 93–95

surprise kits, 7–8

Surprise of the Week, 17

TRAVEL SURPRISE KIT, 8, 130, 164, 188

Nothing-to-Do Jar, 29

Music

brainstorm list and game, 5, 26, 166

dance, 4

GUESS THE SOUNDS AND TUNES, 136, 137, 169

homemade instruments, 4

Microphone Play, 168

records, 4

RHYTHM ART, 78

rhythm instruments, 6

singing, 164

STRUMMING KIT, 79

tape recorder, 136, 137, 169

Parties

birthday cake, 100

cookies, 37, 148, 176

costumes, 4, 41, 45, 62, 70, 114, 116

decorations, 93

favors (see Party Favor Bag, 99)

FIRESIDE KIT, 20, 67, 94, 119

Flame Color Mix, 99

games, 29, 48, 50, 60, 76, 88, 90, 99, 118, 132, 133, 136, 137

gifts (*See* GIFTS)

Halloween (see costumes, SPOOK SALAD MAKING, 104), 131

piñata (see Heidi's Paper Bag Piñata, 98)

refreshments:

    desserts, 37, 60, 98, 100, 106, 109, 148, 176

    DRINKS, 40, 67

    main dish (*See* PIZZA MAKING, 38)

    salad (*See* SPOOK SALAD MAKING, 104)

Science

ACTIVITY AND RECIPE BOX, 14, 102

Bathtub Scientist, 30

Bird Nest Building Bag, 63

BIRD WATCHING, 8, 58, 86, 130, 149

birds:

    identification, 149

    watching, 63, 149, 171

    feeding, 86

brainstorm list and game, 5, 26, 166

collecting, 9, 153, 185

COLLECTION STARTER, 130, 185

Color Play, 133

COLOR TESTER, 164, 172

EXPLORE GRAB BAG, 20, 180

Flame Color Mix, 99

FLASHLIGHT PLANETARIUM, 9, 151

GUESS THE SOUNDS OR TUNES, 136, 137, 169

HEAVY THINGS SINK, 31

Invisible Ink, 30

Light-Up Electric Fun, 133

LOG BIRD FEEDER, 86

MAGNET ART, 32

Magnifying Magic, 134

METRIC SNACK, 16, 80

MYSTERY FEELY BOX, 75

Mystery Smelling Jars, 64

NARCISSUS PLANTING, 69

Nothing-to-Do Jar, 29

PLANT A DESERT, 142

planting:

    African violet, 100

    cactus, 142

    narcissus, 69

Pond Adventure, 63

Pretend Binoculars, 171

PRINGLE'S BUG CATCHER, 9, 82, 131

senses:

    hearing, 78, 79, 136, 137, 168, 169

    smelling, 64

    seeing, 30, 31, 63, 69, 82, 99, 133, 134, 149, 151, 153, 172

    tasting, 97

    touching, 53, 75

SHELL IDENTIFICATION, 10, 153

shells, 153

Spook Salad, 104

straws, 5

TAKE-APART, 15, 53
VEGETABLE SCULPTURES, 16, 25, 26, 28
Violet-by-Mail Surprise, 100

Weather Bureau, 30
Weigh Things, 64
wind, 5, 30

Storytelling

Book Countdown, 169
brainstorm list and game, 5, 26, 166
CLOTHESLINE STORY AND DISPLAY, 84
FELT-BOARD TEPEE, 130, 156
Recording, 136
Microphone Play, 168
MINIATURE SCENE, 7, 94, 140

Mystery Purse, 101
NEWSPAPER BOAT FOLDING, 158
Photo Album, 132
PAPER DOLL AND SET DESIGN, 94, 147
Squiggle Story Notebook, 136
THUMB-AND-FINGERPRINT DOO-
  DLES, 13, 35, 131, 194

Woodworking

bedroom woodworking, 10
boats, 158
CARPENTER'S TOOL KIT, 8, 43
HANG-YOUR-JEWELS HOLDER, 152
Linoleum Block Prints, 27
LOG BIRD FEEDER, 44, 86, 130
MAKE A TABLE, 15, 21, 44, 46
Mini Carpenter, 65

NAPKIN HOLDER, 44, 58, 87
SCENE BUILDING BLOCKS, 60
STOMPERS 'N' STILTS, 125
TAPE RESIST GAME BOARD, 15, 88, 119
Whittling Fuzz Sticks, 62
WOOD PIECES KIT, 154
Work-and-Play Project Board, 135

Appendix II

Activities by Skill

Sensory Discrimination

BAG-OF-LABELS MAKE-A-GAME, 25, 50

COLLECTION STARTER, 130, 185

Color Play, 133

FELT-BOARD TEPEE, 130, 156

FOLLOW THE FOOTSTEPS, 76

GUESS THE SOUNDS AND TUNES, 136, 137, 169

HEAVY THINGS SINK, 31

Map Fun, 132

MYSTERY FEELY BOX, 75

Mystery Smelling Jars, 64

POM-POM MAKING, 16, 20, 33, 58, 115, 130, 165, 166

RHYTHM ART, 78

SHELL IDENTIFICATION, 10, 153

SPARKLING WINDOW SHADE PULLS, 7, 93, 130, 146

SPOOK SALAD MAKING, 104, 131

Spotlight Game, 136

STRUMMING KIT, 79

TAKE-APART, 15, 53

Observation

Bird Nest Building Bag, 63

BIRD-WATCHING, 8, 58, 86, 130, 149

CLOTHESLINE STORY AND DISPLAY, 84

COLOR TESTER, 164, 172

EXPLORE GRAB BAG, 20, 186

FELT-BOARD TEPEE, 130, 156

FINGERPAINT FUN, 66, 130

FLASHLIGHT PLANETARIUM, 9, 151

HEAVY THINGS SINK, 31

Light-Up Electric Fun, 133

LOG BIRD FEEDER, 44, 86, 130

Magnifying Magic, 134

NARCISSUS PLANTING, 69

Pond Adventure, 63

PRINGLE'S BUG CATCHER, 9, 82, 131

ROOT BEER MAKING, 4, 40, 119

SHELL IDENTIFICATION, 10, 153

TAKE-APART, 15, 53

Weather Bureau, 30

Motor Control

Large Muscles

FOLLOW THE FOOTSTEPS, 76

Jump Rope and Jingle Book, 169

LIGHTEN-YOUR-LOAD HELP KIT, 94, 95, 122

MASKING TAPE FLOOR GAMES, 6, 48, 58, 130

OLYMPIC GAMES KIT, 57, 90, 130

PARTY GAME KIT, 16, 94, 119, 120, 158, 159, 192

Ring the Bell, 60

Squeeze Bottle Squirt Play, 29

STOMPERS 'N' STILTS, 123

Tin Can Golf, 29

Small Muscles

BATTLESHIP, 4, 164, 182, 191

CANDY HOUSE, 106, 108

CLIPBOARD PENCIL AND PAPER GAMES, 119, 130, 174, 190, 191

CLOTH FLOWERS, 94, 138

COLLAGE MEMORIES, 103

FAMILY BOUQUET, 20, 95, 110, 131

KITCHEN-MADE SAND ART, 21, 25, 51

NAPKIN HOLDER, 44, 58, 87

NEWSPAPER BOAT FOLDING, 158

PLANT A DESERT, 142

POM-POM MAKING, 16, 20, 33, 58, 115, 130, 165, 166

SPOOK SALAD MAKING, 104, 131

Stencil Art, 167

TAKE-APART, 15, 53

Eye-Hand Coordination

CARPENTER'S TOOL KIT, 8, 43

CROSS-STITCH ON GINGHAM, 130, 165, 166, 177

FLOOR POOL GAME, 118, 119, 130

HANG-YOUR-JEWELS HOLDER, 152

LOG BIRD FEEDER, 44, 86, 130

MAGNET ART, 32

Mini Carpenter Kit, 65

MINI SEWING KIT, 165, 180

NAPKIN HOLDER, 44, 58, 87

PERSONALIZED PENCIL CASE OR BOOK BAG, 105

Rub-On Fantasy, 167

SEWING CARD, 17, 21, 33, 130, 144, 166

SPARKLING WINDOW SHADE PULLS, 7, 93, 130, 146

String a Snack, 170

Whittling Fuzz Sticks, 62

Math Readiness

BATTLESHIP, 4, 164, 182, 191

BEST EVER COCOA MIX, 58, 67, 119, 122

CLOTHESLINE STORY AND DISPLAY, 84

CROSS-STITCH ON GINGHAM, 130, 165, 166, 177

Dice Decide, 168

FELT-BOARD TEPEE, 130, 156

FLOOR POOL GAME, 118, 119, 130

M and M PARTY COOKIES, 16, 37, 115, 164

METRIC SNACK, 16, 80

NAPKIN HOLDER, 44, 58, 87

OLYMPIC GAMES, 57, 90, 130

QUILT-MAKING IRON-ON, 7, 57, 72

SPARKLING WINDOW SHADE PULLS, 7, 93, 130, 146

Unlock!, 171

Weigh-Things, 64

Language Development

Actress Pretend, 62

ARMY-NAVY CAMPOUT PRETEND, 8, 25, 45

BIG-MOUTH DISGUISE, 70, 94

CLOTHESLINE STORY AND DISPLAY, 84

CLOWN, 114

COLLECTION STARTER, 130, 185

DO YOUR THING, 6, 41

EXPLORE GRAB BAG, 20, 186

Listen!, 169

Microphone Play, 168

MYSTERY FEELY BOX, 75

Mystery Purse, 101

NEW NEIGHBOR GET-ACQUAINTED KIT, 165, 179

ROBOT COSTUME, 116

Activities Especially Suitable for Use by Parents, Grandparents, Older Siblings and Sitters, Preschoolers, Teachers, Small Organized Groups, and Day Care Centers

Parents

ARMY-NAVY CAMPOUT PRETEND, 8, 25, 45

Book Countdown, 169

CANDY HOUSE, 106, 108

COLLAGE MEMORIES, 103

FIRESIDE KIT, 20, 67, 94, 119

GOING PLACES SURPRISE, 8, 130, 164, 188

KITCHEN-MADE SAND ART, 21, 25, 51

MAKE A TABLE, 15, 21, 44, 46

NEW NEIGHBOR GET-ACQUAINTED KIT, 165, 179

PAINTBRUSH COOKIES, 122, 148

Party Favor Bag, 99

ROBOT COSTUME, 116

Rub-On Fantasy, 167

Speedy Birthday Cake, 100

STOMPERS 'N' STILTS, 123

TAKE-APART, 15, 53

Work-and-Play Project Board, 135

Grandparents

BERRY-PICKING BASKET, 174

BIRD WATCHING, 8, 58, 86, 130, 149

CARPENTER'S TOOL KIT, 8, 43

CLIPBOARD PENCIL AND PAPER GAMES, 119, 130, 174, 190, 191

COLLECTION STARTER, 130, 185

GRANDMA STOKLOSA'S COOKIE MIX, 119, 122, 164, 176

IRON-ON QUILT MAKING, 7, 57, 72

Jump Rope and Jingle Book, 169

LOG BIRD FEEDER, 44, 86, 130

May Day Pin Basket, 97

PERSONALIZED PENCIL CASE AND BOOK BAG, 105

PLANT A DESERT, 142

POM-POM MAKING, 16, 20, 33, 58, 115, 130, 165, 166

SPOOK SALAD MAKING, 104, 131

TAPE RESIST GAME BOARD, 15, 88, 119

Vegetable Sculpture, 28

Violet-by-Mail Surprise, 100

Whittling Fuzz Sticks, 62

Sitters and Older Brothers and Sisters

Bag of Clay, 96

BATTLESHIP GAME, 4, 164, 182, 191

BEST EVER COCOA MAKING, 58, 67, 119, 122

CLOWN, 114

COOKIE CUTTER KNOX BLOX, 16, 21, 109

Dice Decide, 168

EASY PIZZA-MAKING, 20, 26, 38, 94, 119, 131

FLOOR POOL GAME, 118, 119, 130

Invisible Ink, 30

Linoleum Block Print, 27

Microphone Play, 168

NEWSPAPER BOAT FOLDING, 158

Nothing-to-Do Jar, 29

Patchwork Scribbles, 134

Playdough Marble Roll, 132

Pretend Binoculars, 171

THUMB AND FINGERPRINT DOO-DLES, 13, 35, 131, 194

Tin Can Golf, 29

Preschoolers

ACTRESS PRETEND, 62

Bird Nest Building Bag, 63

Black and Red Cards, 168

Color Play, 133

FINGERPAINT FUN, 66, 130

HEAVY THINGS SINK, 31

Instant Wall Hanging, 65

Listen!, 169

Magnifying Magic, 134

Mystery Smelling Jars, 64

Photo Album, 132

Preschooler's Purse, 170

Pup Tent, 28, 85

Ring the Bell, 60

School Photo Bookmark, 101

SEWING CARD, 17, 21, 33, 130, 144, 166

Spotlight Game, 136

String a Snack, 170

WOOD PIECES KIT, 154

Teachers

ACTIVITY AND RECIPE BOX, 14, 102
BAG-OF-LABELS MAKE-A-GAME, 25, 50
Flame Color Mix, 99
FLASHLIGHT PLANETARIUM, 9, 151
FOLLOW THE FOOTSTEPS, 76
GUESS THE SOUNDS AND TUNES, 136, 137, 169
Map Fun, 132

METRIC SNACK, 16, 80
MINIATURE SCENE, 7, 94, 140
ROOT BEER MAKING, 4, 40, 119
SHELL IDENTIFICATION, 10, 153
Squiggle Story Notebook, 136
Weather Bureau, 30
Weigh Things, 64

Small Organized Groups

AUTOGRAPH CLIPBOARD, 130, 173
BIG-MOUTH DISGUISE, 70, 94
CLOTH FLOWERS, 94, 138
FAMILY BOUQUET, 20, 95, 110, 131
HANG-YOUR-JEWELS HOLDER, 152
Heidi's Paper Bag Piñata, 98
LIGHTEN-YOUR-LOAD HELP KIT, 94, 95, 122
MINI EMERGENCY KIT, 165, 184
MINI SEWING KIT, 165, 180

Mystery Purse, 75
NAPKIN HOLDER, 44, 58, 87
NARCISSUS PLANTING, 69
PARTY GAME KIT, 16, 94, 119, 120, 158, 159, 192
Pond Adventure, 63
PRINGLE'S BUG CATCHER, 9, 82, 131
SPARKLING WINDOW SHADE PULLS, 7, 93, 130, 146
Wooden Spoon Boutique Gift, 96

Day Care Centers

CLOTHESLINE STORY AND DISPLAY, 84
COLOR TESTERS, 164, 172
Crayon Rubbings, 135
DO YOUR THING, 41
FELT-BOARD TEPEE, 130, 156
Light-up Electric Fun, 133
MAGNET ART, 32
MASKING TAPE FLOOR GAMES, 6, 48, 58, 130
MINIATURE SCENE, 7, 94, 140

Mini Carpenter Kit, 65
MYSTERY FEELY BOX, 75
OLYMPIC GAMES, 57, 90, 130
PAPER DOLL SET DESIGN, 94, 147
Pretend Binoculars, 171
RHYTHM ART, 78
Stencil Art, 167
Tissue Paper Stained Glass, 61
Unlock!, 171

Order Form

KITS FOR KIDS and THE PLAYGROUP HANDBOOK may be ordered direct from the publisher,

St. Martin's Press, 175 Fifth Avenue, New York, N.Y. 10010.

Please make check or money order payable to **St. Martin's Press.**

. . . .

Please send_____copies of **KITS FOR KIDS** @ $7.95 plus .75 for postage and handling for the first book, and .35 for each additional book to:

Name:_____

Address: _____

City:_____State:_____Zip:_____

. . . .

Please send_____copies of **KITS FOR KIDS** @ $7.95 plus .75 for postage and handling for the first book, and .35 for each additional book to:

Name:_____

Address: _____

City:_____State:_____Zip:_____

. . . .

Please send_____copies of **PLAYGROUP HANDBOOK** @ $5.95 plus .75 for postage and handling for the first book, and .35 for each additional book to:

Name:_____

Address: _____

City:_____State:_____Zip:_____

. . . .

Please send_____copies of **PLAYGROUP HANDBOOK** @ $5.95 plus .75 for postage and handling for the first book, and .35 for each additional book to:

Name:_____

Address: _____

City:_____State:_____Zip:_____

. . . .